Learning Comes to Life

Related Materials
Available From High/Scope Press

Books in the High/Scope Institute for IDEAS
Program Guidebooks Series

Introduction
Workshops
Work Projects
Room Groups
Evening Programs

Additional Training-Related Materials

Trainer's Guide
Training Study Guide

Adolescent Education Assessment Instruments

Youth Developmental Processes Assessment—YDPA
Job Competencies Assessment—JCA
Youth Program Implementation Profile—YPIP

For information and training in High/Scope's
approach to adolescent education, please contact

Adolescent Division
High/Scope Educational Research Foundation
600 North River Street
Ypsilanti, MI 48198-2898
313/485-2000 FAX 313/485-0704

To order materials,
Phone 800/40-PRESS
FAX 800/442-4FAX

Learning Comes to Life
An Active Learning Program for Teens

Ellen Meredith Ilfeld

With a Foreword by
Karen Johnson Pittman

High/Scope Press
Ypsilanti, Michigan

Published by
High/Scope® Press

A division of
High/Scope Educational Research Foundation
600 North River Street
Ypsilanti, Michigan 48198-2898
313/485-2000, FAX 313/485-0704

Editor: Marge Senninger
Graphic Design and Production: Margaret FitzGerald

Library of Congress Cataloging-in-Publication Data

Ilfeld, Ellen, 1955-
   Learning comes to life : an active learning program for teenagers
 / Ellen Meredith Ilfeld ; with a forward by Karen Johnson Pittman.
      p.   cm.
   Included bibliographical references and index.
   ISBN 0-929816-90-0
   1. High/Scope Institute for Ideas. 2. Socially handicapped youth—Education
(Secondary)—United States. 3. Vacation schools—United States. 4. Active learning—
United States. 5. Group work in education—United States. 6. Project method in
teaching.
   I. Title.
   LC4091.I34   1995
   371.96'7'0973—dc20
                                                                    95-43455
                                                                    CIP

Printed in the United States of America
10 9 8 7 6 5 4 3 2 1

Contents

Foreword

My relationship with High/Scope began in the spring of 1970 when Barb, a dormmate at Oberlin College who knew that I was looking for a summer job, suggested that I apply to be a counselor at the High/Scope summer camp for teenagers. I was skeptical. To a skinny, African-American nonswimmer whose camp experience had been an unsatisfying overnight for inner-city youth sponsored by the D.C. Recreation Department, the idea was not immediately appealing. The more my friend talked about her experience, however, the more I became intrigued. It sounded as though High/Scope was not "fun and sun." The campers certainly had fun, but more important, the campers *and Barb* had had a summer of learning, doing, and reflecting that seemed unique.

Barb's description of the place and program was fascinating—not cabins and swamps, but two grand houses overlooking a pond; not a monotony of games, sports, and crafts, but folk dancing, construction, drama, and physics. Reflecting, however, I now realize that what hooked me was not the richness of her description of the *what* of a High/Scope summer, but the clarity of her explanation of the *why* and the *how.* High/Scope promised and turned out to be a laboratory for helping me answer what have become the driving questions of my career: How can we better help young people set and achieve their dreams? How do we help young people from low-income and minority families beat the odds? More important, how can we create or re-create supports and opportunities that systemically change the odds?

I have reformulated these questions several times over the years. At age 18, the questions were simpler and deeply personal. I was immersed in finding the analytic tools to help me understand why some of the kids and cousins I grew up with had already taken significant detours off the road to success, why some of the blacks on campus closed ranks against nonblack students while others did not. I wanted to understand why people—students and professors alike—were surprised at how well-educated, well-rounded, and "well-adjusted" I was, given my demographics. A budding sociologist, I was already rejecting the theories that I had, in Lisbeth Schorr's terms, "beaten the odds." True, I came to Oberlin with a

D.C. Public Schools diploma, from an all-black community, co-raised by a widowed mother who worked long hours and a godmother who took me into her home during the week. But I did not feel that I had "beaten" anything. I felt that I had been prepared, exposed, encouraged, and rewarded. I felt that I was supposed to succeed and equipped to do so. The idea that luck had more than a small role to play was insulting to me. I wanted to, in sociologists' terms, explain the variation.

Twenty-five years later, I can now explain the source of my frustration with those who praised me, and I can now label, if not prove, the sources of variation. My success was not due to the fact that I had beaten the odds. It was due to the fact that others (family, neighbors, church members, teachers) had changed the odds by offering me a consistent diet of supports and opportunities—and the fact that systems, most notably the schools, had offered me high-quality academic and nonacademic instruction.

This is what young people need—environments (families, schools, religious organizations, youth centers, employers, communities) that offer them consistent, developmentally appropriate diets of supports and opportunities. They also need nurturing, guidance, rules, structures, clear expectations, and consistent limits, as well as strategies for assessing, planning, and achieving goals. And they need opportunities to explore, excel, contribute, earn, lead, join. Services should provide them with high-quality, accessible instruction, care, and settings for positive interaction with peers and adults.

Ultimately, efforts at *prevention* (whether it be prevention of violence, school drop-out, substance abuse, pregnancy, or AIDS) need to include a broader, unwavering commitment to *preparation*. Everyone—all of the institutions and individuals that touch young people's lives—must have this commitment. Narrowly targeted, time-limited prevention programs may help some young people beat the odds, but *it is the quality of the services, supports, and opportunities that are there for young people on a sustained basis that determines what the odds are.*

The High/Scope Educational Research Foundation, through its program development, research, and training activities, demonstrates the wisdom of this commitment. High/Scope is best known for its leadership in early childhood education. For 30 years, it has also worked with teens, developing residential learning environments—first for young people from diverse racial, income, and cultural backgrounds and later for talented disadvantaged youth through formal linkages to schools. Throughout this period, its philosophy, as explained by the author of this book, has remained constant:

> The High/Scope Institute is committed to the philosophy that a multifaceted, rich environment that offers participants the chance to explore, participate in a community, and actively experience new things will foster not only greater academic success but also greater social adjustment. Instead of focusing on dysfunction, programs at the Institute focus on the many positive aspects of teenage development.

In its last iteration as the High/Scope Institute for IDEAS, the program for teenagers has a solid and impressive evaluation-base that demonstrates the breadth and sustainability of its impact. The program is residential, but the lessons learned can easily be applied to nonresidential schools and youth organizations. They can also be applied to treatment centers and to programs run by housing authorities.

The message is simple but forceful. Adolescents grow up in environments. The adults in those environments can profoundly influence the pacing, direction, and evenness of adolescents' growth if they understand four things:

- *The dimensions of development:* Adolescents are growing not only physically but also socially, emotionally, intellectually, morally, sexually. Growth is uneven among and within adolescents.

- *The dynamics of development:* Development does not occur without engagement. Young people must be challenged (on all fronts) and encouraged to express their own ideas and respect others', to define their own problems and solutions, to develop their own divisions of labor.

- *The demands of development:* Adults must learn to be partners with adolescents. Development is not taught. Adults can facilitate; can encourage and support; can observe, listen, and help reflect; can participate. They cannot, however, make development happen. Similarly, they cannot make development *not* happen.

- *The dilemmas of development:* Development occurs as much during nonstructured time as during structured time. Encouraging young people to use their nonstructured time in ways that support reflection and appropriate interaction with peers is key.

Anyone taking the time to read this book will understand these facts in a way that they have not understood them before. They will also appreciate both the enormous potential of young people and the enormous effort it takes to respond to that potential 24 hours a day. *Learning Comes to Life* is simultaneously a case study, a literature review, and a guidebook demonstrating that there is a *science* to helping young people reach and use their potential. Its strength, for practitioners and policymakers alike, is its specificity. It describes, from wake-up to lights out, what it takes to create an environment that supports adolescent development. It paints, through the words of students and staff, how that environment looks and feels.

The High/Scope Educational Research Foundation has something to say that this country needs desperately to hear: Ordinary young people can be primed for success through careful and consistent attention to their environments. We need to listen. I spent three summers as a counselor at High/Scope, and I have spent 25 years building on that experience; I am excited that now others, through *Learning Comes to Life*, will have the opportunity to share it. I am especially delighted that Ellen Meredith Ilfeld, one of "my" campers, has put her intellect, heart, and imagination into writing this book.

KAREN JOHNSON PITTMAN

Karen Johnson Pittman was the music counselor at High/Scope's summer camp for teenagers from 1971 to 1973. A graduate of Oberlin College and the University of Chicago, she has devoted her career to policy research, public education, and advocacy on youth issues. She reconnected with High/Scope four years ago, when she was director of the Center for Youth Development and Policy Research, which she founded in 1990. Karen is currently Director of U.S. Programs for the International Youth Foundation.

Acknowledgments

My four summers at High/Scope camp (the forerunner of the High/Scope Institute for IDEAS) were the most meaningful experience with community and with learning that I have ever had. Twenty-four years after being a camper, I find that I still feel the effects of those times. Thanks to David Weikart and his vision of active learning, I relate to music, art, dance, architecture, science—all creative ideas and performances—with the eyes and ears of someone who as a teenager had the good fortune to act, think, create, build, brainstorm, and experiment with a wide range of media. Thanks to Phyllis Weikart and her gift for teaching folk dance, I feel comfortable moving my body in space—in concert with the rhythms of music, other people, and even other cultures. Whenever I am in a group situation, I catch myself monitoring the group process: Is everyone's input being heard? Is the group brainstorming creatively and letting ideas flow? Is the talk being grounded in concrete plans for action, realistic experiences, artistic expressions?

Through the years of its camp and Institute, High/Scope has distilled some very special approaches to working with teenagers, to creating active learning experiences, and to helping young people develop group skills that will serve them throughout their lives. It is in thanks for being part of that process and for the ways this experience continues to enrich my life that I wrote this book.

Thank you in particular to David and Phyllis Weikart for their energy and hard work in overseeing the creation of this approach to working with teens. Mary and Charles Hohmann also had rich input. So did dozens of bright college students, many of them from Oberlin College, who brought the best of their experiences to add to the mix. Karen Pittman, who contributed the thoughtful Preface, was among them. She was a great camp counselor and is one of the many exciting role models/friends who continue to stay connected to High/Scope in a professional capacity.

Nicole Yohalem, the Director of the High/Scope Institute for IDEAS at the time this book was being written, was invaluable in furnishing materials, giving advice and insight, and helping the project to move along. Alberto Rodriguez, Aura Weinstein, and the rest of the High/Scope Adolescent Division staff also generously contributed their insights and experience. Sherri Oden of the High/Scope Research Division posed good questions and gave helpful feedback. My colleague Judith Evans offered much-appreciated thoughtful comments on the first draft of this manuscript. Thanks to all of them.

In the High/Scope Press production of the book, I'd like to thank Marge Senninger for her patient editing under pressure; Lynn Taylor, Editor-in-Chief; and Margaret FitzGerald, the book's designer, for her attractive cover design and layout.

Introduction

I t is impossible to experience 50 years of summer camping with young people without being deeply committed to what such residential programs for youth produce for all who are involved. Serving either on staff or as program director, I spent the summers of my high school and college years (from 1946 to 1958) at five different camps in Ohio, New York, Maine, and Michigan. Once I had completed college (interrupted by a stint in the Marines), I served in yet another program—Camp Rising Sun, a scholarship camp for boys near Rhinebeck, New York. Since those years, I have had responsibility for the High/Scope residential program for teenagers, which began in the early 1960s as a summer camp program and has now evolved into the High/Scope Institute for IDEAS.

In a very real sense, this series of camp experiences was a developmental odyssey for me. The early years took me from maintenance and kitchen work into counseling roles and finally into responsibility for program operation and staff supervision. At one point, however, in 1958, I did find my interest in the camp experience beginning to wane. By then I had learned how to organize a good entertainment and sports program while keeping campers and staff safe and involved. But I still saw camp programs as having mainly recreational value.

Then, in the late summer of 1958, at the suggestion of a friend, I visited Camp Rising Sun. This opportunity was a formative experience for me. I realized that it was possible for a summer residential program to include a far broader range of activities than is typically offered by a recreational or specialty camp. I saw that a program could be effective in engaging minds, in opening paths to greater self-realization, and in creating the opportunity for a demanding commitment to both self and peers. For adolescents, such an experience produced not only a good time but also an occasion for deep personal change; not only participation in planned activities but also ownership of ideas, friendships, and new skills at all levels. Wanting to be part of such a program, at 28 years of age I joined the Rising Sun staff and soon found myself involved at a new and deeper level of responsibility, as camp director. Thus I renewed my commitment to a field that had already contributed so much to my own personal development.

Buoyed by my experience at Rising Sun, in 1963, together with my wife, Phyllis, I established the High/Scope summer camp program. During the first several years, we were assisted by John and Jane Salcau and Pete and Ida Kingston—the men were colleagues from the Ypsilanti Public Schools, and the camp could not have been established without them. The camp was designed to serve talented youth, regardless of social class or ethnic background. It was founded on the belief that if each adult uses his or her own special skills to work with adolescents, all of us are well served. Young people then have the support essential for their normal growth and development. Operating an effective camp program was the special skill that I was prepared to offer young people.

But programs for youth don't just happen——it takes care and effort to develop a service, systematically implement it, and maintain high-quality delivery year after year. From my experience with High/Scope program development at all levels, I am convinced that *using a model approach* is essential to maintaining high quality. The basic principles behind the High/Scope model approach to adolescent programs are these:

1. Adolescents need a safe psychological environment in which to explore new styles of thought, social behavior, and personal challenge. Young people who have developed a reputation of being "good" in one specific area often hesitate to explore new opportunities or difficult tasks, either because they fear failure or because they see the new challenges as unrelated to what they can already do comfortably. "I don't do math" or "I never could write" are typical comments one hears from self-conscious adolescents. They need a setting where failure to solve a problem or fulfill a plan in a new area does not bring negative judgment from adults or derision from peers.

Adolescents' cautiousness about trying new social behaviors is even more evident. On this front, the forces that keep personal initiative and exploration in check range from the threatening language of urban street gangs or the loud derogatory slang of the sports field to the whispered "insider" gossip of school halls and cafeterias. If behavioral changes are disdained, if attempts to contribute to the total group are mocked, or if efforts to include everyone in a circle of friends are rejected, it is understandable why many teenagers resist accepting new and demanding personal challenges.

    2. Adolescents need a chance to make new beginnings. In spite of their reputation for liking adventure, teenagers can be creatures of habit, hemmed in by all sorts of pressures. If parents have placed pressure to conform to specific behaviors or dress, in rebelling against this, the young person may fall into even more rigid habits of behavior and dress as dictated by the code of the streets or by popular fashion. Indeed, modern commercial culture stands ready and willing to dictate teen behavior, dress, attitudes, food, drink, and music. An effective program provides teenagers with an opportunity to be free for a time from whatever pressures have formed their existing habits. The program offers alternatives: new adults to relate to, new peers as friends, a new personal schedule, a change in food, and freedom from the trappings of popular culture. All of this amounts to an opportunity for new beginnings. Young people are able to test their increasingly adult minds and bodies in new ways without the baggage of living up to (or living down) what they were before the program.

    3. Adolescents need program activities that are designed to relate to their stage of development. Watching movies and TV programs gives us all a false sense of what teens can accomplish (we only see the best, the odd, the different—and not the typical). An effective program for young people allows them to select activities that will permit some degree of success. But whereas adults usually want adolescents to excel at what they try, adolescents themselves frequently want to be able to just relish the experience. Instead of wanting to be an acclaimed actor in a school play, a young man may simply want to enjoy the camaraderie of being in a play without bringing down criticism on himself; instead of wanting to excel at playing a musical instrument, a young woman may be satisfied to experiment with goofy harmonies on the piano. Having spent the early adolescent years getting their body ready for adult growth, learning to think abstractly like adults, and gaining a modicum of social skill with peers and the family, teens, especially by ages 14 and 15, seem to need time to simply interact with tools and materials, with language and ideas, on their own terms; achieving excellence may not be a primary concern. A good program allows the *possibility* of achieving excellence without including the *demand* that it be achieved. When teenagers have choices about what they do, are surrounded by varying degrees of excellence in the work of others, and are supported by adults who understand their developmental needs, true growth can and does occur.

4. **Adolescents need to have genuine responsibility.** Helping a teenager to sense that he or she is a responsible member of a community, capable of addressing the tasks of that community, is one of the major contributions of an effective adolescent program. As families lose their rural connections and as less time is spent around the home with maintenance and construction projects, teenagers of both sexes have fewer chances to develop comfort with using implements and tools and doing work that requires physical skills, exertion, and perseverance. Furthermore, when their school experiences include little or no hands-on learning, it is no surprise that young people would rather talk about a problem than carry out a plan of concrete action to resolve it. They often do not see a job to be done, or if they do, they may have little idea of the effort it involves and little sense that they can accomplish it. A good adolescent program can do something about this. It includes opportunities for young people to be responsible and contributing leaders and participants in ways that benefit the program's entire community. It helps teenagers to see that what they learn and experience in this "ideal" community can carry over into their home community. In a good program, *responsibility* does not mean simply doing as you are told or following the rules—that is obedience. True responsibility is understanding what is needed by fellow group members and helping to meet that need. A high-quality program provides the framework in which adolescents come to realize such a sense of responsibility.

Ellen Ilfeld, who in the 1960s experienced the High/Scope program first as a student participant and then as a staff member, alludes to these four basic principles throughout this book. She includes information from the model program she knew in the 1960s, and yet, in all of its essentials, it is the same model program that exists and thrives today as the High/Scope Institute for IDEAS.

Many of the anecdotes and scenarios Ellen uses in this book describe happenings at some of the most recent sessions of the Institute. It is reassuring to see that because of the power of using the model approach, despite a span of 30 years, there is congruence between recent accounts and Ellen's early experience with the High/Scope program. As one who has been privileged to be part of this program over that entire 30-year span, I hope this book will convey to readers the immense value of giving adolescents the foundation they need to become contributing members of tomorrow's world.

DAVID P. WEIKART
PRESIDENT
HIGH/SCOPE EDUCATIONAL RESEARCH FOUNDATION

In the fall of 1995, the United States Department of Education's Program Effectiveness Panel (PEP) certified the Institute for IDEAS for inclusion in the National Diffusion Network (NDN). The Institute for IDEAS is now identified as one of a select group of exemplary programs that have been field tested, thoroughly evaluated, and proved effective in improving student performance and that lend themselves to a variety of educational settings. PEP certification is a nationally recognized standard among educators, and the NDN is the only system of its kind in the country. The IDEAS program can now be promoted by NDN facilitators in each of the 50 states, the District of Columbia, Puerto Rico, the Virgin Islands, Guam, and American Samoa.

Learning Comes to Life

1

The High/Scope
Institute for IDEAS Program—
Its Beginnings and Evolution

At eight o'clock on a warm May evening, 50 teenagers between the ages of 14 and 17 have gathered in a converted barn to go shopping. Their instructions are simple: They will each receive 50 "ducks" to use for their shopping spree. They have 30 minutes to decide what they will buy, and they are to keep track of their purchases on a slip of paper they carry around with them. The "wares" are noted on cards posted all around the meeting room, each with the price in ducks listed below it. The organizers of the activity make sure that everyone understands how to proceed:

"Any questions?"

"Can we buy whatever we want?"

"As long as you don't spend more than your fifty ducks."

"Can we buy on credit?"

"Your ducks are credit. And your limit is fifty."

The group disperses. Some individuals proceed methodically, taking notes. Others race randomly from card to card, examining the possibilities: a slick new car, a cheaper but serviceable jalopy, dinner with your favorite star, new clothes, the magical ability to do well on SATs, an evening with someone from history, lessons on the musical instrument of your choice, psychic powers, a permanent free pass to the fast-food chain of your choice. . . . There are 30 items in all, ranging in price from 2 to 30 ducks.

Across the barn on the far wall, different types of items appear: world peace, 450 ducks; a cure for AIDS, 300 ducks; quality housing for all, 200 *ducks; an end to domestic violence, 270 ducks; no more drug addiction, 300 ducks; quality education for all students and higher pay for teachers, 200 ducks.*

There is a buzzing as the shoppers reach these new cards and realize there is something wrong: They don't have enough ducks for these higher priced items. Stephanie, who is 14 years old but frequently acts much younger, is the first to come up with a solution. She runs up to one of the organizers of the activity to ask if she can pool her ducks with other people's. This is the first time since she arrived here that Stephanie has offered a constructive suggestion in a problem-solving context.

"Of course, as long as you each limit your expenditures to fifty ducks."

Stephanie is off to spread the word, oblivious to the fact that she has had a small breakthrough in her style of contributing to the group.

Now the bargaining has begun in earnest. Several groups of shoppers have formed for brief meetings near the new cards. There are several students moving back and forth from one group to another. Participants take notes, tally expenses, and figure out their budgets.

One striking feature about the groups is their mix, which is not typical for teenagers. The African-American, Hispanic, and Caucasian participants are all together, and such high school distinctions as "nerds," "populars," and "jocks" are obviously immaterial in this context. A 14-year-old African-American girl from inner-city Detroit, who is usually quite shy, is bargaining intently with a 15-year-old boy from a rural all-white setting who has a tough-guy demeanor. They are joined by three other shoppers who would never be "caught dead" with either of them in the regular school context. But everyone is absorbed in the task, and this breakthrough moment also passes by, as just another normal aspect of the experience.

When the 30 minutes have passed and shoppers are standing around in groups chatting, reconfirming some of their bargains, the entire group reconvenes. The organizers invite participants to talk about what they have chosen and why. They ask the group: "How do you want to discuss this— randomly, by room group, or by going around the circle?" The shoppers quickly come to a consensus, deciding to listen to each person consecutively around the circle, offering individuals the right to choose not to share.

Most of the shoppers have split their ducks between the lower priced personal items and the higher priced humanitarian ones. As each person shares his or her criteria for making choices, certain patterns begin to emerge, which the shoppers discuss:

"I used Duwayne's strategy of trying to get as many different things as I could afford."

"I went with Melody and put half my money into one big thing I wanted and half into helping other people."

There are some surprises: One tough Detroit youth, whose persona includes dressing well and talking about fast cars and slick possessions, chose to use all his ducks to purchase a cure for AIDS. "I have an uncle with AIDS," he explains.

Several of his peers look at him with surprise, since this is the first evidence of a serious side to his personality. "That's great you'd do that," one of his friends says. "I wish I'd thought of it."

The group finishes reporting on individual purchases and spends a few more minutes commenting on the overall experience. The participants note that they have collectively managed to buy all the big-ticket items but one: an end to the war in Bosnia. ("Where is Bosnia anyway?" someone asks.) They agree it feels good to have collectively bought most of the humanitarian items. They take a moment to congratulate themselves on having a social conscience.

Then the student organizers suggest singing a good night song. Everyone stands and joins hands in a circle. Once again, it is notable that around the circle, the group is united. Differences of race, age, status, and gender have taken a back seat to what is paramount in this moment—a sense of shared community and shared experience. Most people's eyes scan the circle as they sing. The song is broken into three parts to create a round learned earlier in the day, and the group breaks into spontaneous applause at the end. Their voices have created a beautiful effect in this large room, and they say good night to one another, feeling extremely pleased with their accomplishments.

• • •

The opening vignette describing a typical *evening program* at the High/Scope Institute for IDEAS conveys the sense of sharing and community that each Institute student experiences. Multiply this positive experience by 30 days, by 16 different program periods each day, and by 58 individuals, and the magnitude of the opportunity for engagement that is available to teenagers at the High/Scope Institute for IDEAS begins to come clear. Though the 450 program hours of the month-long Institute are equivalent to a semester of school time, the community setting intensifies the experience. It allows for some unique kinds of interaction and engagement among students. They influence one another in many positive ways and make important breakthroughs in their social, emotional, and intellectual development.

The History of the Institute for IDEAS

Over the past 30 years the High/Scope Foundation has developed this residential learning environment into a dynamic experience for teenagers. Working first with a summer camp for capable youth and later with a month-long residential program for talented disadvantaged youth, High/Scope has created an approach to working with young people that supports their emotional, social, and intellectual development. It helps individuals to realize their potential.

High/Scope's work with youth began in 1963 with a camp program directed by High/Scope Foundation President David Weikart and his wife, Phyllis Weikart. He was at that time a psychologist working with the Ypsilanti public school system, and she was a physical education instructor at the University of Michigan.

The initial High/Scope program was neither a typical camp nor a school. It was an *experience in creating a community* for youths 12 to 17 years old and also a *laboratory* for engaging in active learning. Situated in southeastern Michigan on an old 380-acre farming estate, the program provided teenagers with a new setting in which to live and work with others, to actively pursue ideas and interests, and to use a wide range of intellectual and physical capacities.

The program has always operated within an *open-ended framework*. This framework makes it natural and enjoyable for teenagers to actively explore tools, materials, and ideas. It allows them to identify their own interests and concerns throughout the learning process. Learning is integrated with interactions; thinking and problem-solving skills are developed in the context of real situations.

Over the years since 1963, Dr. Weikart's original "summer camp for capable youth" has continually evolved. In 1974 responsibility for program operation was assumed by the High/Scope Educational Research Foundation, and the camp became a seven-week workshop, with a continuing policy of tuition subsidies for participants (including full scholarships for almost a third of the students). The program attracted an international, interracial, multicultural mix of participants.

Actively exploring materials, tools, and ideas enables teenagers to identify their own interests and concerns throughout the learning process.

In 1981 the program was adapted to meet the growing national challenge to address the needs of disadvantaged youth. Now a one-month version of the program, called the High/Scope Institute for IDEAS, serves as a residential academic enrichment experience for selected low-income high-potential students. Cooperating high schools release the students from school, so they may participate in this residential, intensive experience.

At-risk teenagers are not the only ones who deserve opportunities for building self-esteem, however, and the residential camp setting is not the only place where the lessons learned from the work at the Institute for IDEAS can be applied. All teenagers can benefit from the chance to function as whole individuals, which means the chance to

- Learn in settings that challenge them to use social, physical, creative, and emotional faculties as well as intellectual ones

- Participate in groups formed for collaboration rather than competition, where every individual's contribution is valued

- Learn to interact purposefully with peers and to initiate constructive activities

- Learn to communicate with peers of both sexes as real people

- Express themselves verbally, physically, and creatively in nongraded, nonjudgmental, purposeful settings

- Learn how to work at tasks using their minds, bodies, materials, and tools

- Have opportunities to both define the problems they deem worthy of attention and use their creative and intellectual abilities to address them

- Meet and get to know people who serve as inspiring and accessible role models

In other words, all teenagers deserve what a session at the Institute for IDEAS offers: an opportunity to use their energies and talents in integrated ways and also to contribute their energies to a larger community effort that benefits them collectively as well as individually. The following scenario describes how an Institute session typically begins.

• • •

Early Morning Arrival

All teenagers deserve an opportunity to use their talents in integrated ways and to contribute their energies to a larger community effort that benefits them collectively as well as individually.

Breezes are blowing as the bus pulls into the driveway on a cool day in May. The staff can hear the excited voices of the students (who refer to themselves as campers) even before they see the bus. The group consists of 30 talented disadvantaged students, 14 to 16 years of age, from inner-city Detroit. Most of them are African-American; some are Hispanic. Many of these young people have never been out of the city before. Most have never been away from their families for more than a few days. All have agreed to leave behind many of the distractions of their youth culture: cigarettes, radios, popular music, drugs, cars, TV, weapons, alcohol. A few of them are returning students who have explained to the others just what this place is like. Most of the participants are arriving with the vague expectation that it will be fun and different, and that they will learn some new things.

Later this morning a second bus will arrive from northern Michigan with an additional 28 students who have been selected from a multicounty rural school system. They are all Caucasian, or white; some have never even met people of other races or cultural backgrounds. They too are talented but disadvantaged, have never been away from home, and have agreed to leave behind the trappings of their teen culture.

Staff members have already been here for a week undergoing an intensive training program. The staff are 14 recent college graduates with a variety of interests and talents, and their training has been active. They have systematically engaged in program exploration, group exercises, physical tasks, and community-building activities. They have had a chance to become thoroughly familiar with the facility and materials available to them; they have collaborated on planning program activities and practiced the instructional approach in introductory sessions with one another.

Staff members have learned a repertoire of songs and folk dances that will serve as an integrated part of the "shared culture" that evolves within the community. In addition they have lived together in a cohesive atmosphere that will allow them to support one another in their work with the students. They have followed a modified version of the daily routine for students, getting a feel for the pace and focus of the various program elements. They have experienced the transformation from being strangers to becoming part of a community, a process they will now apply in working with the students.

As the Detroit students climb off the bus, some of the unique features of this group are already evident. They are made up almost equally of boisterous, highly social types, who in the two-hour bus ride have established fast friendships, and quieter, often shy people, who seem to be dazed or overwhelmed. One couple—a "bus match"—emerge holding hands.

Staff members introduce themselves and help to organize the arrival. They locate the students who will be in their respective room groups. (Rooms hold from four to six students; two large houses accommodate the boys and girls separately.) They show students to their rooms, help organize *a brief stowing of luggage, and lead them back to the dining hall for registration. The goals during this time are to help students feel comfortable, to orient them to the physical surroundings, and to encourage them to make friends. Staff divide the participants into small tour groups led by returning students. These tour groups will then be responsible for orienting the students arriving on the second bus. All students are later given an introduction to High/Scope activities in an afternoon program.*

Afternoon Program

Working in four pairs, staff members have designed sample activities in cooperative games, music, construction, and drama. Students are divided into four groups that rotate through these activities, which are located at separate stations. As each group spends approximately 30 minutes at each station, students have a chance to sample some of what the Institute has to offer. The activities are carefully planned to be recreational, interesting, and low-pressure; students can participate quietly, taking in the experience individually, or they can begin to develop relationships with their peers; some students can even begin to emerge as leaders in various capacities. The following accounts illustrate a typical first-day activity in each of the four stations.

The Game Station

Tony is a calm, low-key leader, which is helpful for students who are experiencing first-day fears and shyness. After asking students to stand in a circle, he explains this cooperative game: Everyone is to think of a food item that starts with the first letter of his or her first name. Tony gives an example and then asks for a volunteer to start the game. The object is to go around the circle and have participants link their names with alliterative food items (Pam—Pomegranate). Each participant says his or her name and food and then recites the names and foods that came before, all the way back to the original person. Tony wants this game to be fun as well as helpful, so he's conscious of not putting people on the spot. When one student, Rachel, gets stuck on a name, he waits a moment to see if she'll recall it, then gives her a hint instead of allowing her to get flustered or embarrassed.

After this activity the group seems warmed up, so Tony brings out three tennis balls. He begins tossing one ball around the circle, explaining that the object is for the receiver to be able to say "Thank you _____ [naming the student who tossed it]," and then to call to someone else, "Here _____ [naming the student it's then tossed to]." Tony starts the ball in action, and the group gets moving. Once a rhythm is established, Tony adds two more balls to the game, and things start to get silly. Students laugh as they must run to retrieve overthrown balls at the same time that they are trying to get a smooth pattern going. At the signal to move to the next station, students are still laughing, they are familiar with the names of some of their peers, and many first-day tensions have been relieved.

The Music Station

Jim has chosen to teach a first-day song in parts, which the whole group will later perform together at the evening program. Many of the students in the first group he encounters are already enthusiastic about music. A couple of them spontaneously break into harmony. Picking up on that, Jim helps them figure out ways to organize the piece. The two "spontaneous harmonizers," a 15-year-old girl from northern Michigan and a 16-year-old boy from Detroit, step in to organize the others in four-part harmony. They agree to meet later with Jim and two other students, who volunteer to figure out how best to organize the whole community after dinner for a repeat performance of the song.

The Construction Station

The task here is to create a group mobile. Each student is given a set of materials that includes some sort of adhesive (tape, glue, rubber cement, stickers) as well as several small pieces of balsa wood, some paper, and a variety of small hardware (nails, screws, bolts). Sara, one of the staff, adds that students are welcome to collect any other materials from outside that they wish to use. Certain tools are available for their use, provided that a staff member has confirmed their familiarity with safety precautions.

Students are asked to contribute something that represents themselves in some way. This leads to discussions about what individuals have selected and why. Several students show that they have a serious side, though it is clear that most of them are not used to sharing insights about themselves in a mixed setting. The activity also provides students with an opportunity to investigate the materials available in the shop and art areas, which will be useful during the evening program.

The Drama Station

Several students arrive at this station saying "I can't act." Susan breaks the ice by inviting everyone to join in a theater game. Standing in a circle, each person is like a cog in a machine. The first person mimes an action; the second person picks up on the action, modifies it, and then passes it on to the next person; each person adds his or her modification as the action passes around the circle.

Juan and Susan are using this activity as a warm-up for the main goal of the drama station, which is to perform one of four acts of a first-day play that was written for this specific purpose several years ago by a group of students. Each act has several speaking roles and also several chorus parts, so students who are not comfortable speaking alone in front of the group can get up on stage in a safe atmosphere. This first group will learn the first act; each following group will go through warm-up activities and also learn an act. Students will read from scripts, so no memorization is necessary. At the end of the afternoon the whole group will come together and perform the play. Only hours after arriving at the Institute, the participants will experience (and create) a whole-group performance that is quite impressive.

First-time staff members and students are often surprised at how quickly the process of active engagement and community building begins. By dinner time students are already "present"—visibly involved—though many are quieter than they will be when they know one another better. They have already caught on to much of the routine and to the expectations of enjoyment, experimentation, exploration, and cooperation that characterize every aspect of the program. As a result of the afternoon's name games, the room-group arrangements, and the assignment of students to table groups, students are well on their way to knowing everyone by name and feeling at home in this new environment.

Staff members have already established a low-key leadership style in which their role is to introduce program elements, help students start interacting, and then let them actively explore activities on their own. Each student has already participated in multiple groupings. Some of these (like room groups) have been designed by staff to facilitate intercultural exchange, and others have been determined by program choices, random chance, and individual interest. Students have been exposed to a variety of activities, pursuits, and collaborative experiences that they are not likely to encounter in their routine academic settings.

Evening in Community

The first day ends as each day does, with a whole-community evening program. This first evening, students are invited to create "personal crests." Gathered together in the barn on a huge dance floor, participants are again divided into small groups of seven or eight, designed by staff to mix ages, races, national origins, and gender. Working within this context, the groups decide which themes to use for their crests (common themes include goals, hobbies, achievements, fears, and special role models); they then determine which materials they will need to bring to their work space from the art and shop areas and from the natural setting directly surrounding the barn. After a ten-minute period of gathering materials, they begin to create their individual expressions of the chosen themes.

Once the crests are completed, all the groups reconvene to share what they have created. Each group presents a summary of the elements they discussed; individuals from each group show the crests.

The evening program ends with a group song. Teaching a simple round based on a haiku, Kevin, one of the two directors, helps bring the attention and energy of the group into a quieter, focused moment of sharing. Standing in a circle and singing together, students begin to experience a sense of community. They begin to form bonds with those they will be interacting with in hundreds of ways over the next four weeks.

In their rooms again, getting ready for bed, students discover that the High/Scope experience does not end with the close of the formal program. Rather, students are encouraged to think about things they might do together as a room group during the upcoming weeks, such as reading poems together, taking short camping trips, writing a group story or song, or designing an activity for self-scheduled time *(a time—called SST— in the daily routine that is strictly for student-led or -initiated activity). Students are encouraged to find ways to explore and express their group energy, avoiding cliques and exclusivity. As a way to recognize and integrate the changes that each student experiences as a participant in this special kind of community, individual students are encouraged to share their reflections of this first day.*

The High/Scope Educational Philosophy

The High/Scope approach to education enables young people to awaken to themselves as learners, to become active participants in and shapers of their own development, and to define as well as solve problems. Academic success is greatly enhanced when students have confidence in themselves, have identified their own motivations, and have experienced themselves as successful learners in a variety of situations.

As applied to adolescents, the High/Scope educational philosophy incorporates five key components: choice, active participation, plan-do-review, cooperative learning, and leadership. These components are an integral part of the community living and the learning activities of the Institute for IDEAS.

Exploring concepts intellectually should not be the exclusive mode of learning. Adolescents need opportunities to use their bodies as well as their minds.

Choice

Students must feel that they have real choices in what they do, how they participate, what their focus of interest will be, and what goals they set.

Active Participation

Adolescents need to be able to use their bodies and their minds in learning. They also need to work actively with materials and tools. Although they are certainly able to sit and listen and to explore concepts intellectually, this should not be the exclusive mode of learning. All individuals thrive when given opportunities to be actively engaged in tasks that challenge them to use all their faculties.

Plan-Do-Review

It is important for young people to follow a conscious process of learning that encourages them to

- *Plan*—plan the goals, approach, steps, and schedule of a specific task

- *Do*—initiate action by gathering information, making choices, proposing initiatives, taking risks in executing a plan, and carrying out that plan

- *Review*—reflect on the progress or outcome, examining the effectiveness of their attempts, revising their plans for future efforts, and relating or presenting the experience to others

Cooperative Learning

An important developmental feature of the adolescent years is the need to participate in social exchanges and to explore issues of membership and belonging. Negative collaboration, which often takes the form of peer pressure to conform, squelches individual initiative. But positive collaboration, in work, play, and academic studies, enables students to develop a more broadly grounded sense of their ability to contribute to collective tasks and problem solving. Cooperative learning projects offer students the opportunity to achieve more extensive goals than they might achieve indi-

Cooperative learning builds self-confidence by offering students opportunities to achieve more extensive goals than they might achieve individually.

vidually. This builds self-confidence. Most if not all activities at the Institute are structured to encourage collaboration, which strengthens each student's sense of competency and community spirit.

Leadership

When students are collaborating regularly on tasks that range from the most mundane and physical to the most abstract and academic, there are numerous opportunities for each individual to shine. These multiple opportunities for leadership, coupled naturally with the necessity to learn other fruitful ways to participate, enable all students to develop leadership skills. Students learn to become aware of the needs of the whole group; they develop the ability to move among various roles and various levels of group participation.

TAKEN TOGETHER, these five elements form the basis of High/Scope's approach to working with teenagers. They are relevant in all interactions between adults and teenagers. Whether adults are helping students to complete a work task, to share living spaces effectively, or to grow academically, each individual's development is greatly enhanced by the opportunities for authentic choice, active engagement, a plan-do-review process, cooperative learning, initiative, and leadership. The scenario that follows illustrates how these key components play out in the active learning that typically occurs in a week at the Institute.

● ● ●

"It feels like we've been here two weeks already!" Monette announces the fifth night at dinner. The students in her table group all nod in agreement. They feel as if they have experienced more in these five Institute days than they would have in five days back home. They have, *in fact, had more experiences. The schedule has been a full one, and there has been much opportunity for student-initiated activity and little time for unfocused "hanging out." The other reason why Monette's experience feels so intense is this: Like her fellow students, throughout the past five days, she has been engaged in all of her activities. She has not been a passive observer.*

Early in the week, Monette chose to join a group of students whose work project *was to build a water wheel to generate electricity to light the bridge. One of her contributions to the project was to notice that the paddles needed to be contoured to catch the water more effectively. She volunteered to make a model, and the group decided to ask a staff member to help them create the model on the computer. Although she had little experience with computers, Monette decided to go along with the small delegation undertaking this task. By the end of an afternoon session, she had mastered the basics of the modeling program and was debating with her fellow builders the merits of three different designs.*

Monette also attended a club (one of the shorter instructional units) on mask-making, tramping all over the fields in search of natural materials to use as symbols for the various elements of the mask that the group had decided to make. Students in this club were so excited about the masks that they decided to use SST to organize a play using them; they would offer the play at the next musicale performance.

The day that Monette's table group was responsible for mess duty, she took over the task of washing pots and pans. A friend in the photography club has taken pictures of Monette on duty, as proof for her mother, who will find it hard to believe that Monette is working and enjoying it.

About midweek Monette took a big risk and joined a basketball game. This was a real switch for her, because basketball games back home are so rough that she never dares to join in. The High/Scope version of the game is like everything else at the Institute—designed to accommodate all levels of skill. She confessed her fears to the group, and they explained that the newly created court rules required the more skilled players to collaborate with the less experienced ones. They also cheered her on, even when she was clumsy.

In the span of only five days Monette has learned more than 20 folk and traditional songs and has gotten past her shyness about singing after meals. Yesterday she actually stood up and made a presentation to the whole group about the computer-modeling session. When several students asked to see the designs, she ended up demonstrating what she had learned to four other people.

Monette has made several new friends, and in some ways she feels closer to them than to the kids back home. Some of these new friends are white, which surprises her, since she associates only with African-American kids at her school. Her room group has discussed how much they have had to adjust their preconceptions and prejudices since they got here. They talk about trying to put together a video next week that they can show to friends back home about racial myths and prejudice.

She has spent her self-scheduled times this week down in the shop, learning to use the various tools and working to become certified on the lathe. She was taught by Mike, a big-boned, somewhat inarticulate, white teenager from northern Michigan, who turned out to be pretty nice. She told her room group that she was in shock. She never in a million years imagined herself learning to use tools, talking to someone like Mike, actually getting to be friends with someone like him.

Monette's table group has had both similar and different experiences so far at the Institute. She has heard reports of their activities from each of them. She has compared notes with others in her room group. She has seen countless student presentations after lunch and dinner each day, so even when she is not directly involved, she feels a part of the new ideas and activities and possibilities going on around her.

Monette is participating in a wide array of new experiences. It is new for her to be confronted by choices repeatedly during the day. It is new for her to be continually engaging in various activities rather than hanging out day after day with the same group of friends or parking herself in front of the TV. It is new for her to feel so much a part of things, without having to work to be a member of the "in group." It is new for her to talk so much in front of her fellow students. Normally she is fairly quiet at school. But this doesn't feel like school to her, and so she is discovering a new side to her character.

This morning after breakfast, staff members made small presentations on the upcoming workshops *they will be offering. Unlike the four-session clubs and work projects this week, each workshop will consist of nine sessions lasting an hour and three quarters apiece. Staff members hand out to everyone a sign-up sheet of available workshops, assuring students that they will receive their first or second choices. Students also are given the following descriptions of the first set of workshops offered at this Institute session:*

- *Architects and Others . . . Using only balsa wood and string, we will build model bridges that will hold 30 pounds of weight or more! We'll get ideas by exploring existing bridges and other structures around camp. How does that suspension bridge really work? Come find out, and build your own!*

- *Las Fallas. Combine sculpture and social activism. Las Fallas is an ancient festival from Spain in which huge fallas, floatlike papier-mâché sculptures, are built to represent social problems. We will build fallas representing problems in our own society and will close with the traditional nighttime burning of the fallas, symbolizing solutions to the problems.*

- ***And the Survey Says . . .*** *Are you curious about your fellow campers? We will create our own social survey to give to the rest of the Institute community, collect data, and interpret the results. To join, you don't have to be a research scientist—just curious!*

- ***Stained Glass.*** *Come down to the woodshop and learn how to transform pieces of colored glass into a wonderful stained glass sculpture. All you need to bring is your creativity and a bit of patience.*

- ***Panopticon.*** *If you're interested in journalism, creative writing, editing, or graphic design, come join the newspaper group. We'll be laying out the paper using computer desktop publishing. This is a "time capsule" you can take home!*

- ***Homemade What?*** *Do you have a pencil or a pen but nothing to write on? Have you ever thought about making your own paper? We will make our own paper that can be used for stationery, creative writing, card-making, or anything you want. We will also put together our own books, with paper we make ourselves.*

- ***Sound and Silence.*** *How do you hear things around you? What is sound? Come tune in and open your "ear-lids" to the exciting world of deep listening. Sound voyages, computers, music, and building our own primitive instruments will fill our workshop days. The project will reach a crescendo in a group composition and/or performance.*

- ***Monologues.*** *Do you like to talk? Then this might be the club for you. When actors have long speeches, they often reveal significant aspects of their characters. This can be one of the most challenging experiences for an actor. We will be developing and fine-tuning monologues for presentation.*

Monette has chosen the workshop called Stained Glass. From her perspective it sounds like fun, and she would like to create something to take home to her family. Jim, the staff member who is offering this work-

shop, works hard to make the experience enjoyable, but he also has a little more in mind.

Jim and other staff members work hard to create and organize challenging activities that will allow for collaboration as well as individual initiative; actively engage each student at his or her own level of understanding and skill; and offer opportunities for exploration, choice, problem solving, and fun. Accomplishing all this while maintaining a nondirective stance is the challenge faced by the Institute's young teachers.

Instruction at the Institute for IDEAS is student-centered, which means that the staff's role is to inspire, facilitate, support, and reflect students' progress—not to dominate, direct, or determine. Although the staff members have received thorough training during the week before students arrive, many of these young teachers were educated themselves in a more traditionally academic, curriculum-centered environment. Thus, it is an ongoing challenge for them to master the planning and facilitating skills that allow active, student-centered learning to flourish. To meet this challenge, staff members meet regularly throughout the month of the Institute to share plans and ideas and to encourage one another.

• • •

Participants in the High/Scope Institute for IDEAS often describe their experience as one of freedom. As one student put it, "You are free to discover who you are and what you like to do. High/Scope is a place where you can be real, and people will respect you for being yourself." Ironically, this freedom is possible because of the carefully planned environment. Freedom at the Institute is not formless; it is the result of a carefully designed open framework that includes

- A flexible yet predictable schedule.
- Social expectations that encourage individual awareness of the larger community and promote the creation of shared culture over individual achievement or glory.
- Creative use of a variety of materials and opportunities for physically active endeavors.
- Consistent, clear support from adults, who are trained to

create, recognize, and offer opportunities for student engagement and leadership.

- Role models who work with students during all waking hours and in a variety of contexts; who offer constant exposure to new ideas, interdisciplinary thinking, social/emotional and intellectual problem solving, and other living-learning skills.

- An active, "team" staffing process that regularly takes into account the needs and progress of individual students. Problems are addressed through careful program planning and coordinated staff strategies that create a strong, positive community experience.

The overall goal of the program is to create an environment that is both psychologically and physically safe. In an unsafe environment—one that is inconsistent, arbitrarily authoritarian, physically dangerous, socially exclusive, or emotionally unsupportive—teenagers easily get trapped in reactive behaviors and antisocial activities that alienate them from themselves, from each other, and from the larger community. In a *safe* environment, however, adolescents can learn, take risks, grow, make mistakes, support one another, test friendships, establish good will, trust others, and form meaningful relationships with adults.

Benefits of the Program: Short-term and Long-term Implications

The High/Scope Foundation has worked with many populations of adolescents over the past 30 years. Program participants have ranged from talented and financially comfortable middle-class students to socially disadvantaged "at risk" students, and experience has shown that nearly all teenagers benefit from the combination of *a clear consistent framework* and *constant, diverse opportunities for choice and individual initiative.* In particular, students who did not experience consistency or autonomy in their home environments were able in many cases to discover new abilities and self-confidence in the High/Scope Institute environment.

In 1991, High/Scope's adolescent program became a national model of academic enrichment. With the support of a leadership grant from the DeWitt Wallace–Reader's Digest Fund of New York, this program has been replicated (with variations) in several other locations across the country.

Research on the High/Scope Institute for IDEAS, funded largely by The Ford Foundation, The Skillman Foundation, and the Detroit Edison Foundation, has begun to identify some of the educational and social benefits of participation in the program. Compared to High/Scope's longitudinal research on preschool effectiveness, the research on our work with adolescents is still in the early stages. Nevertheless, a preliminary five-year longitudinal study (Oden, Kelly, Ma, & Weikart, 1992) shows that students identify the Institute as an important and positive influence on their attitude toward school and social participation. Compared with their counterparts in a similarly selected control group, significantly more alumni of the Institute, especially those considered nonachievers in their high schools, attend 2- and 4-year colleges. Also, greater numbers of Institute alumni enter the military, and for low-income students this often leads to postsecondary education. The study also found that Institute participants whose parents hold low educational expectations for them (which is often a correlate of low achievement) are more likely to overcome their parents' negative views and go on to postsecondary education. Experiences in the month-long High/Scope program apparently give students a higher estimate of themselves and allow them to become less reliant on parental assessments of their potential. Institute participants also tend to cite a wider spectrum of role models, including Institute staff, successful peers, teachers, and other nonfamily members.

Through its landmark High/Scope Perry Preschool Project (Schweinhart, Barnes, & Weikart, 1993), which is a longitudinal study of children from their preschool years to age 27, the High/Scope Foundation has demonstrated the lasting effects of a high-quality preschool program. The study found that an enriched environment appropriately supportive of children's developmental needs has benefits to society that go far beyond academic success. The benefits to the High/Scope Perry Project preschoolers, who are now adults,

include fewer arrests, greater financial self-sufficiency, more mar-
riages and accompanying births within wedlock, and more home
ownership. The benefits to society as a whole include a savings of
$7.16 for every dollar spent on programs for young children, as well
as the security of developing adults who contribute to society rather
than drain its resources.

At this stage of our adolescent program research, we cannot
yet claim that the High/Scope Institute for IDEAS has an equally
far-reaching influence on its participants. But we can propose, from
our extensive experience and research with children and adults, that
exposure to a developmentally appropriate, rich environment does
positively affect youth. It affects them both academically and socially.
If we want to create adults who are engaged actively in their work
and communities and are able to collaborate with others, then it is
useful to let teenagers learn in a setting that supports such active
engagement and collaboration—where these experiences are natural
and enable students to achieve both personal and group success.

2

Who Are the Participants and What Do They Need?

Matt is a 16-year-old from a small town in northern Michigan. His tough exterior and somewhat aggressive appearance (various body piercings, a Mohawk hairdo) seem to demand distance, respect, and perhaps fear. However, his warmth and need for support and companionship surfaced almost immediately with the few staff and peers whom he trusted.

Matt is a talented artist, a fact he reveals slowly, over time. Though art clearly is his avenue for expression, it is a strength that seems to have gone untapped in his school or at home.

Matt often gets into trouble at school. In fact, he jokes about spending more time in the office than in the classroom. He is an extremely smart guy who seems to be unchallenged by the approach and content of his school curriculum. Two things at the Institute caused him to flourish: the depth of experience he had, particularly in the arts, and the strong bond he developed with a favorite staff member.

When given an opportunity to share his skills with others, he was a capable teacher and a caring mentor. Matt was also a storyteller. He fascinated his room group with nightly accounts of his feats and adventures and was always anxious to respond to questions or share details. He liked to achieve a shock effect (perhaps it was a means to get attention at home). One of his most memorable attempts was the occasion he used his time in the art area to tattoo himself with a safety pin. When he showed everyone his tattoo at lunch, his handiwork was received with neither shock nor approval; it did result in a talk with the Institute doctor about the health risks involved.

Matt had a special interest in national politics, and he slammed the Washington administration whenever he got a chance. He had hilarious moments and extremely serious ones as well, often just a few minutes apart. For example, in listing his goals for the program, he wrote, "I hope this experience will help me understand more clearly the differences between myself and others," and then a few sentences later, "I want to be the Grand Monarch of Terra for all eternity." (From the Institute Director's notes)

● ● ●

Matt, the student described in the opening vignette, is in many ways typical of the teenagers at the Institute for IDEAS. They are full of contradictions: They can be individualistic yet conforming, savvy yet naive, serious yet silly, personable yet defensive. Although it is helpful to look at the demographics of a group of participants to get some idea of the developmental characteristics involved, the Institute students always demand—and deserve—to be seen as individuals with unique needs and requirements.

Over the years the demographics of those served by the High/Scope Institute for IDEAS have shifted. Disadvantaged youths have always been included, but the original camp program mostly attracted middle-class young people, who were often from homes where intellectual achievement was highly valued and where exposure to arts, culture, and ideas was ongoing. Of course, the early participants included some students who were succeeding academically but not developing social or practical abilities, as well as some who were bright and talented but rebellious and failing to reach their full potential. Since High/Scope has always emphasized diversity, a quarter to a third of the participants came from several sponsoring schools abroad and from various low-income U.S. locations (Hawaii, rural Mississippi, inner-city Detroit). Travel was financed partly by a student-run apple orchard, and some students received full scholarships to attend.

Staff at that time were drawn from Oberlin College, the University of Michigan, and a variety of other colleges and universities. They too were bright, independent-minded, and talented, and some, like the student participants, had experienced mixed success in their own earlier academic years. As "near-peers" between the ages of 21 and 26, they had much to offer the students as role models and mentors. Yet because of their own transitional status, they too were still in the process of sorting out their gifts and abilities.

Staff members were (and continue to be) highly creative students, educators-in-training, or recently graduated young professionals. Supporting this young staff are one or more adult directors with experience in programming and education. This three-tiered combination of youth, young adults, and more-experienced adults has proved effective: The near-peer staff are able to offer highly energetic, enthusiastic programming in a way that is not threatening or alienating to the teenaged participants. The adult directors are able to provide support and experience, so it becomes an active learning environment for the staff as well as the students. This has proved to be an effective way to create a dynamic, engaged community.

In the past ten years the High/Scope Institute for IDEAS has expanded its demographic focus, adding sessions that are sponsored by school systems and that serve young people who live in impoverished conditions. The students in these sessions largely come from households where the parents or adults do not have much formal education themselves and do not promote academic or intellectual achievement. Many of these teenagers have experienced disruption in their families through divorce, displacement, or exposure to alcoholism or violence. Most of the Institute participants come from economically disadvantaged homes; about half are high-achieving students and half are students with low to moderate school grades. All participants, however, are young people who have shown some indication of high potential for achievement.

Staff members for these new programs are usually recent college graduates; some come from backgrounds similar to the participants'. Their varied expertise in arts, applied science, and other program areas is bolstered by an expressed interest in youth development. But they are still educators-in-training, near-peers, role models, and mentors, and they are aware of their role in helping to expose participants to new ideas and activities and helping to create a sense of community.

Typically, programs designed for at-risk youth focus either on providing intensive (sometimes remedial) academic work or on counteracting specific problems, such as teen pregnancy, drug abuse, or delinquency. The High/Scope Institute is committed to the philosophy that a multifaceted, rich environment that offers participants the chance to explore, participate in a community, and actively experience new things will foster not only greater academic success but also greater social adjustment. Instead of focusing on dysfunction, programs at the Institute focus on the many positive aspects of teenage development.

High/Scope research bolsters our commitment to this philosophy. Although the High/Scope Institute does not teach academic subjects in a consistent, sequenced way, it has positively influenced the participants in their academic outcomes: As explained in the last chapter, more Institute participants go on to higher education; more who make it to college are persistent in pursuing a college education; and more enroll in the military, which offers them an avenue to further training. Institute alumni cite the program as a major positive influence in their lives, and they are more likely than others to overcome negative parental attitudes or low expectations about their academic achievement (Oden et al., 1992).

The philosophy that at-risk youth will benefit from an enriched, "whole" experience is rapidly gaining credence among youth development specialists, and it is reinforced by what is known about the developmental needs of adolescents. This makes logical sense. Why shouldn't economically disadvantaged youth benefit from programs that have been successful with more-advantaged young people, *if the programs are sensitive to the cultural backgrounds and social realities of their participants?*

Just as Head Start is able to make a difference in the lives of young children by appropriately supporting their development, programs for teenagers can also make a difference if they appropriately support adolescent development. In the insert "Student Goals" on pp. 30–31, several Institute students describe what they hope to accomplish at the High/Scope Institute. Their descriptions illustrate the diversity of developmental needs within individuals and among teenagers within a two-year age span.

A Brief Overview of Youth Development

Although it is possible to identify several key developmental changes that are common to most young people—their bodies change, they grow more capable of abstract thought and reasoning, they become focused on their peer group and on their community—it is also true that there is great variation from one teen to another. Moreover, most of the research on the needs and characteristics of teenagers has been conducted with middle-class Caucasian subjects and may not apply equally to youths from disadvantaged homes or from other racial, ethnic, or cultural groups.

With this in mind, we find it useful to consider the development of adolescents on three levels:

1. Their general developmental traits or characteristics

2. The tasks and developmental gains characteristic of the young people at the Institute

3. The needs of young people during adolescence

Developmental Characteristics

Teenagers between the ages of 12 and 17 often vary greatly in their physical, intellectual, and emotional abilities. As J. M. Tanner, a physician who specializes in adolescents, put it, "To speak . . . of a 'boy aged 14' is to be vague to the point of leaving out almost everything that is important about 14-year-old boys. The same is true of talking about 12-year-old girls (or 13-year-old boys or girls, naturally)" (Tanner, cited in Dorman & Lipsitz, 1984, p. 3).

Sometime between the ages of 10 and 17, most teenagers experience rapid physical growth and development, which alters their self-image and appearance to others. This growth includes the onset of puberty, with the appearance of secondary sexual characteristics and a shift in hormonal patterns that can affect some (but not all) teenagers' moods, nutritional needs, and energy levels. Teenagers' physical development can greatly affect their social, emotional, and cognitive development, as well as the way in which they interact with others. As Dorman and Lipsitz pointed out, "It is perfectly normal for one 13-year-old to be physically mature and look like

STUDENT GOALS

Early in the Institute session students are asked, "What is your goal for this week? What do you want to accomplish by the end of the Institute session? What are your goals by the time you finish high school?" Here are some of their responses, which demonstrate rather poignantly some of the developmental contradictions of adolescents as they struggle to find their place in the larger world of peers, school, and adulthood:

Rachel: (1) I want to learn how to crochet in the next week. (2) During this session I want to learn new things like how to use power tools and build things. (3) By the time I finish high school I want to get my pilot's liscense [sic] and also keep my hair braded [sic] for most of the next three years. Why? I don't know, and a scholarship to college.

Meliya: (1) Lead a fishing group. (2) Want to do something or make something I can take home or show to all the campers. (3) Join an engineering program and come back to High/Scope.

Solly: Have a dance for staff and kids. Build a couple things in shop class. Move out of this state.

Tamara: Have a dance, loose [sic] weight, have kids.

Jamie: Have a dance, look better, have a job, and get a diploma.

Stephany: (1) Lose 20 pounds. (2) Lose 40 pounds. (3) Be a size 6 at my prom.

Karen: My goal: to learn as many new things as I can. Another goal: same as above. Goal to accomplish by the time I graduate high school: ???

Andy: (1) For my goal I would like to meet more new friends, and learn more new things, but I would especially like to learn to play the guitar. (2) For the next two weeks, I would basically like to do about the same and maybe more. (3) Throughout high school I would like to get real good grades, meet new friends, and learn more about becoming a draftsman, and learn more about the arts and music, and maybe write something meaningful.

an adult, while another, also perfectly normal, looks like a child" (Dorman & Lipsitz, 1984, p. 3).

Many theoreticians—including Erikson (1963; 1968), Sullivan (1953), Piaget (1972), and Bronfenbrenner (1979), in whose work the High/Scope philosophy is grounded—have described adolescence as a time in human development when one defines himself or herself

Samantha: (1) In the next week, I want to have a goal of assisting the Fancy Drill team, [making] more friends, and helping other people. (2) I want to accomplish a better attitude, experience, and liability. (3) I want to get all my credits I need, participate in the big sister/brother club, help people more often, and become the vala-victorian [*sic*] in my class.

Jim: (1) To find out everyone's name and get to know everyone else very well. (2) To make something for mother. (3) Get a job and have enough money for College U of M.

Chrystal: (1) Finish my picture frame, learn how to drill, learn everybody's name. (2) Get to know people better, learn songs more. (3) Be an exchange student.

Joe: To get to know everyone better. Get some official sport started like football. Get letters in football, basketball, baseball, go all state in football.

Noah: I want to make some kind of project in woodshop before the end of next week. I want to be good friends with everybody here, and to become more serious and less playful. I want to have accomplished better study habits for college, a better relationship with people, and to become more focused on learning.

Ally: (1) Be able to do a musical or something of that sort without worrying about what other people are thinking of me. (2) Learn how to finish a friendship bracelet correctly. (3) Bring my grades up to my highest potential. Be more open with my talents.

Brenda: To overcome stage fright! To let people know that I'm nicer than I look or than they think. I want to have my driver's and cosmetology licenses.

John: Try to contribute in helping with the life-gaurad [*sic*] chair. Try to cut down on sugar intake. Try to come back to High/Scope.

as an individual with an identity that is apart from the family but in growing relationship to society, specifically to the community. In American society, the peer culture for teenagers is perhaps the first proving ground where choices are made in reaction to and apart from adult culture. "A Profile of Steve" on p. 32 describes one student's experiences in defining himself with his peers at the Institute.

A PROFILE OF STEVE

Steve is a 15-year-old student from northern Michigan. When he first arrived, many staff members assumed that dealing with his adjustment to the Institute would be a challenge. Although Steve was outgoing and friendly from the moment he got off the bus, he also happened to be the largest and heaviest of all the students. Very likely a target of ridicule among his peers in high school, he looked like what many teenagers would quickly label a "nerd." It was all too easy to imagine ways his peers might react to him, given the emphasis that teenagers place on appearance.

Although some students initially responded in predictable ways to Steve, he was always a full participant in activities, and he soon stood out because of his unique personality and his aptitude for coining witty phrases. It was not unusual to see Steve with paper antennae rising out of his hat in imitation of a favorite "Star Trek" character. Nor was it uncommon to hear him deliver a humorous announcement after lunch. For example, one day he warned everyone about the noisy stair he wanted the guys to avoid during *siesta*, so he wouldn't be awakened from his daily nap. In addition to having such amusing habits, Steve also often reached out to his peers—asking those who looked sad whether they "felt OK," or making sure that all members of a group were heard and included in a discussion.

Steve taught his peers (and perhaps even staff members) a lesson about prejudice. As people got to know him as the bright, sensitive, and witty person that he was, they seemed to realize how cruel prejudgments can be. The Institute environment provided Steve with opportunities to demonstrate his fine social qualities, and many students rethought their tendency to dismiss peers who were "uncool" or different, based on appearance or superficial acquaintance.

It is possible that the painful role Steve played in his high school's social hierarchy made him the extraordinarily sensitive and friendly person that he was. He may have had a special awareness of how it felt to be excluded or ridiculed. If this was the case, it was entirely to his credit that he responded by being positive rather than bitter or negative toward others. In the course of the month, he became an unusual role model to most and a solid friend to many.

In designing program activities at High/Scope, several key factors of adolescent development are addressed. Because this period is characterized by its rapid changes, we provide a program full of choices that allow students to feel safe to explore and experiment with their changing understandings of themselves and the world around them. Research from Piaget and others (e.g., Keating, 1990; Case, 1985; Vygotsky, 1978) indicates that the adolescent's ways of evaluating choices are influenced by his or her growing cognitive capacities—especially by the increasing capacity for higher levels of abstraction and scientific reasoning. We have found that teenagers' emerging ability to use abstraction and higher order thinking skills is best supported and nurtured in a concrete context: when they are solving the problems presented by an engrossing task or when they are examining the issues related to an engaging activity.

Teenagers' development of abstract thinking skills is best nurtured when they are engaged in tasks that require problem solving, decision-making, and communication.

We have also observed that higher order thinking does not just miraculously appear in adolescents. Rather, adolescent thinking is influenced by the level and types of problem solving, decision making, and communication processes typically employed in family and school situations. Some adults never fully develop the ability to use abstract thinking. Research suggests that the more a young person is called on to use these abilities, the more likely he or she is to develop them (Keating, 1990).

The cognitive abilities that psychologist Jean Piaget called formal operational skills appear to be like language: All people have the capacity to develop the skills, but the *extent* to which they develop particular skills depends in large part on exposure, interaction, and use. As Keating (1990, p. 59) observed, "The import of much of the research is that supportive contexts and early attention to the development of reasoning are precisely what is required to increase the likelihood of its emergence." Keating went on to affirm that the Piagetian legacy, in which the High/Scope approach is rooted, "benefits current work on adolescent cognition. The emphasis on adolescence as a transitional period in cognitive development remains justifiably influential. In addition, much of the systematic data on developmental differences in performance on a range of cognitive tasks derives from this approach."

In summarizing the evidence to date on adolescents' cognitive growth, Keating (1990) pointed to the following characteristics of students in this stage:

- Greater cognitive capacity, facility, and knowledge, with ease in coordinating differing mental representations

- Increased awareness and openness to diverse resources

- Spontaneous use of strategies for gaining and applying knowledge in planning, considering alternatives, and solving problems

- More self-reflection and monitoring of one's own thinking

- Recognition of uncertainties and relativity, coupled with exploration and search for knowledge

Since we at High/Scope believe that the capacities listed above develop in large part in response to opportunity, the Institute for IDEAS responds to each of these characteristics in its programs:

Greater Cognitive Capacity, Facility, and Knowledge, With Ease in Coordinating Differing Mental Representations

The Institute supports the development of this skill by providing students with opportunities to design and build structures in the construction area, to write and enact dramas, to create works of art, to resolve social issues that arise within the community, to use computers to model possibilities, and to share their perceptions verbally and experientially with one another.

Increased Awareness and Openness to Diverse Resources

This skill is fostered as students interact with a variety of role models; as they use tools, materials, and programming elements to try new things; and as they put their ideas into action.

Spontaneous Use of Strategies for Gaining and Applying Knowledge in Planning, Considering Alternatives, and Solving Problems

This characteristic is addressed throughout the student's day, in both academic and group-living elements of the program. Students are asked to plan, work cooperatively, and respond to open-ended tasks by choosing their own approach and coordinating it with group efforts.

Engaging teenagers in planning helps them become aware of and take responsibility for their thinking processes and development.

More Self-Reflection and Monitoring of One's Own Thinking

This ability develops naturally as students are asked to follow a plan-do-review sequence in all that they do. It is further strengthened through community interest, as students have repeated opportunities to present their ideas and activities to one another, to brainstorm in groups, and to reflect on their experiences, both in the context of activities and in a more social context, such as when they are at dinner or in their room groups.

Recognition of Uncertainties and Relativity, Coupled With Exploration and Search for Knowledge

Development of this capacity is supported by the open-framework setting of the Institute, where curriculum is not a preset body of knowledge but a flexible, active, exploratory process. This process is brought to life by each individual student and by each group of students as they interact.

In their development, teenagers vary as much intellectually as they do physically; furthermore, in a single individual there can be great swings of maturity in thought processes from one moment to the next and from one topic to the next. This variation in development was well illustrated in the student goals (given earlier in this chapter, on pp. 30–31). Consider Rachel, for example, who on the one hand wanted to get her pilot's license and on the other hand wanted to keep her hair braided for three years! Many adolescents still lack experience with *concrete thinking* in diverse practical contexts, and so for them, abstract lessons about these topics make little sense.

In terms of their social and emotional development, people tend to become increasingly aware of themselves and the world around them. At this stage of development, they begin to focus on their peer group and their relationships. For example, almost all of the students quoted on pp. 30–31 mentioned at least one goal relating to social relationships. However, many traits commonly identified with adolescents' social and emotional growth, such as the development of relationships with the opposite sex, are actually related in large part to cultural expectations. Thus, in thinking about the traits of adolescent development, it is important to be aware of and sensitive to cultural differences among various ethnic groups.

Also it is important to keep in mind that some of the traits ascribed to adolescents—especially the negative traits—actually apply to only a small percentage of teens. As Dorman and Lipsitz reported,

> Much of our thinking about adolescence is influenced by the myth that adolescence is necessarily a period of storm, stress, and outright rebellion. Recent studies of normal adolescents and their families show that the social and emotional problems generally

associated with adolescence have been greatly overemphasized. In reality, 80% of all adolescents make it through this time of great change without undue turmoil. Of that 80%, about one-quarter experience continuous, serene development; 35% experience development marked by surging starts and stops, childishness one day and adult behavior the next; about one-fifth develop in a turbulent manner that is not abnormal or pathological; and about one-fifth do not fit into any of the subgroups but their tendency is toward continuous or surging development (Offer, cited in Dorman & Lipsitz, 1984, p. 3).

For the remaining 20 percent, who exhibit what the literature calls serious disturbance, there is not yet enough evidence to determine whether developmental difficulties are due to physiological factors or social influences or both. It is possible that if all teenagers were given an opportunity to develop in a supportive and safe environment, this percentage would be significantly lower. Whether developing in a serene or stormy manner, many teenagers are not able to develop to their full potential; many lack sufficient safety in their social and academic settings to interact, to explore, and to take risks without worrying about their image or their grade point average.

The theoretical writings about the developmental traits of adolescents do not provide an adequate picture of the realities experienced by individual teenagers. Thus, an understanding of common developmental traits is helpful but should not be the only information to use when developing a program for teenagers.

Tasks and Developmental Gains

In *At the Threshold*, Elliott and Feldman (1990, p. 12) define the core developmental tasks of adolescents as "becoming emotionally and behaviorally autonomous, dealing with emerging sexuality, acquiring interpersonal skills for dealing with members of the opposite sex and preparing for mate selection, acquiring education and other experiences needed for adult work roles, and resolving issues of identity and values." They modify this definition by reminding readers that ". . . superimposed on these old issues are for many a set of new problems . . . "

Among the teenagers who attend the High/Scope Institute for IDEAS, financial restrictions pose challenges and limitations. Many, in the absence of consistent adult attention, must parent their siblings and themselves. Many must cope with a lack of physical or psychological safety, which prevents them from focusing on who they are and what they want. Many have not had the time for or the privilege of being a child—they have not been taken care of or had the experiences our culture assumes children or dependents are due. Some have been so alienated in their school settings that they cling to childish behaviors that block development of autonomy and self-awareness. "A Profile of Mindy" shows some of the struggles one Institute participant experienced in trying to establish her identity while struggling with an unstable family situation.

Although emphasis on academic success and adult responsibilities increases during the adolescent years, teenagers also need opportunities to have fun.

Teenagers in today's society are exposed to the adult world and adult concerns with increasing frequency and insistence. More and more parents and educators are concerned that popular music, TV programs, and movies present violent and stereotyped versions of the adult reality. Many young people experience their school as a cultural vacuum that is quite separate from their life in the larger community and that does little to support their ethnic identity or culture.

Increasingly, students are being pressured to chart a life path early on and to fulfill specific curricular expectations. (This can be seen in the trend toward state mandates that spell out the types of

A PROFILE OF MINDY

On first meeting Mindy, one could easily take her to be much older than her 14 years; she appears mature, articulate, and confident. She seems at ease in new situations and ready to volunteer for positions of leadership or responsibility.

It wasn't until spending a day or two with Mindy, however, that Celia, her room counselor, realized that her qualities of confidence and leadership were only part of her very complex personality. Mindy soon demonstrated that she had a lot of trouble listening to others and engaging in a mutual conversation. Her peers quickly became discouraged by her inability to listen and her tendency to talk nonstop in almost any situation. Her behavior was additionally challenging because, unlike most students, she didn't seem to hear when peers or counselors tried to give her feedback about her domineering personality.

In room group activities and through late-night conversations, Celia began to see that Mindy's behavior was neither random nor a lack of consideration for others. She spoke often and at length about her parents' divorce and about her feelings about her parents. Her sharing of the pages of poetry she had written about the divorce revealed painful and unresolved feelings. Celia could recognize in the stories and poetry that Mindy was trying hard to make sense of experiences that were very difficult to understand. Mindy was struggling with questions that weren't easily answered, questions that left her feeling unsure about herself in some fundamental ways.

Once Celia understood the link between Mindy's aggressive approach to communication and her lack of confidence, she was able to help many of the students to see beyond Mindy's annoying behaviors. She was also able to find ways to help Mindy overcome the tendency to dominate conversations. Celia found that engaging Mindy's energies and creativity in projects was helpful. Despite her lack of social grace, Mindy was bright and talented. Students who at first reacted negatively to Mindy were eventually able to develop respect and appreciation for her talents. Mindy was especially fond of performing, and this provided an appropriate outlet for her interest in being the center of attention. She impressed staff and peers alike with her individual performances of poetry and her participation in a group theater piece.

By the end of the month, most of Mindy's peers had found effective ways to relate to her. She did make friends, and some of the more mature students were helpful in integrating her into groups.

knowledge students must acquire in their middle school and high school years.) Students are being told that the academic path is crucial to success in this society, and the alternatives that used to be offered through vocational training are becoming less accessible.

In this atmosphere, in the face of adult expectations and requirements for academic achievement, the developmentally appropriate tasks described by Elliott and Feldman are being put aside by many young people. They simply lack the time or the appropriate setting to be transitional, changeable, experimenting teenagers. In this context, an enriching experience like the High/Scope Institute for IDEAS can fill a real social, experiential gap for adolescents, as well as serve as a model for modifying and reforming academic settings.

The developmental tasks that teenagers need to address can be grouped into three areas: *those that are mainly characteristic of being a teenager,* such as becoming adept at teen culture or developing a stronger identity and self-image; *those that involve making the transition from child to young adult,* such as striving toward increased autonomy and turning to peers for validation; and *those that reflect preparation for adulthood,* such as being concerned about vocational plans and academic achievement (derived from Pittman & Wright, 1991).

Most academic programs for youth focus on the tasks that prepare them for adulthood: developing good study skills, learning a work ethic, and assuming increasing responsibility. But teenagers are more successful in preparing for adulthood if they are also supported in their transition from childhood, if their whole self is validated and supported, and if they are helped to find positive ways to form a unique culture and community with their peers.

Adolescents appear to thrive when they are able to *evolve* from childhood to adulthood in a safe context—when they are allowed to make mistakes, to "try on" various behaviors, and to be themselves—in all their complexity. "Three Student Profiles" describes how some recent Institute students began to thrive in a new setting.

Development takes place in a *context,* as adolescents react and respond to the people and situations around them. Youths who have grown up with consistent, fair, responsive parenting and a culturally rich and safe environment are fortunate, because they are supported in the normal tasks of adolescent development. Other adolescents,

THREE STUDENT PROFILES

Mary hasn't had much time to be a child. As the oldest of seven—with a single parent, an alcoholic father—she has spent most of her time being a mother to her siblings and worrying about keeping the family together. Mary is very sweet, sometimes too sweet, and will yield her desires to anyone in the group. It has been a big sacrifice for her to dare to be away from her family for a whole month, since she is not convinced that her brothers and sisters will get fed or be attended to in her absence. An aunt and uncle have assured her that they will help out, but Mary worries every night, losing sleep. During the day, she often drags around, unable to concentrate on her activities. The staff has been especially solicitous of her, and she seems surprised. It has begun to dawn on her that perhaps she can be helped and supported too. Her room counselor has begun to talk with her room group about collaborating on tasks—helping and allowing yourself to be helped.

• • •

Mike seems oblivious to his surroundings. He has been to the infirmary four times already for injuries that came from tripping over things or walking into walls! He says that at home no one ever pays any attention to him, and indeed, he often appears to think he is invisible. Yesterday when students were sharing ideas around a circle, he had a moment of great awakening as he realized that he expected people to just skip him. He stuttered and stumbled over his opinion (he hadn't bothered to formulate one). Finally, one of the other students suggested that they ask him questions to help him figure out what he thought.

• • •

Jenny acts like a little girl, giggling, disrupting conversations, leaving her belongings all over. Some of the students complained that it was hard to have a decent conversation around her, because she kept trying to break it up. Yesterday, in a drama workshop, the group decided to assign Jenny the role of the mother. She doesn't have a mother, and so the group agreed to coach her in what a mother acts like. It has brought up a lot of interesting conversations about what a parent's perspective might be. It is the first time that Jenny has been quiet and has let others talk. She seems to be drinking in the information.

however, grow up in a disruptive, unstable environment, with the pressures of poverty, adult insecurity, and sometimes violence. These young people also need to be offered a consistent, fair, culturally rich environment in which they can safely experiment with being themselves. It is in this experimentation that they develop a positive sense of self, create intimate and trusting relationships with others, and learn to think and act effectively.

The Needs of Young People During Adolescence

Pittman and Wright (1991) cited these needs of 10- to 15-year-olds:[1]

1. *Diversity:* the need for a wide range of experiences to accommodate large variations in development in this age group;

2. *Self-exploration and definition:* the need for opportunities for informal discussion, exploring the world around them;

3. *Meaningful participation:* the need to use their talents, assume responsibilities;

4. *Positive interaction with peers and adults:* the need to work with peers in small groups, pairs, teams; opportunities for being with non-family adults;

5. *Physical activity:* the need to exercise and move (programs must recognize the large differences in size and ability);

6. *Competence and achievement:* the need for a variety of opportunities for success and reward, opportunities for service to others;

7. *Structure and clear limits:* the need for clear rules and structures which they have had some role in developing. (p. 22)

When the Institute's context and approach are described in Chapters 3 and 4, we explain how these seven needs are addressed throughout the daily routine, not only in what students do but also in how each activity is addressed by staff.

Calling them "Desirable Youth Outcomes" (see p. 43), the *First-Year Report* on the Professional Development of Youth Workers listed a similar set of needs. Written by an advisory group of the Office of

DESIRABLE YOUTH OUTCOMES

MEETING NEEDS

Young people have basic **needs** critical to survival and "psychosocial health." They need a sense of

- **Safety**—Perception that one is safe, physically and psychologically; that there exists adequate "structure" in life

- **Self-Worth**—Perception that one is a "good person" who is valued by others and by self

- **Mastery and Confidence**—Perception that one is accomplished and has abilities valued by self and others; that one has some control over daily events

- **Autonomy/Independence**—Perception that one is a unique person with a history, present, and future; that one can "make it" in the world

- **Closeness/Affiliation**—Perception that one loves, and is loved by, kin and fully appreciated by those with whom friendships are formed

- **Self-Awareness/Spirituality**—Perception that one is intimately attached to larger systems; identification and affiliation with a cultural group, higher deity, or philosophy

BUILDING COMPETENCIES

To succeed as adults, youth must acquire adequate attitudes, behaviors, and skills. Important "competencies" are

- **Physical Health**—Good current health status and evidence of knowledge, attitudes, and behaviors that will assure future well-being, such as exercise, good nutrition, and effective contraceptive practices

- **Mental Health**—The ability to develop and maintain a personal sense of well-being, as reflected in the ability to analyze and reflect on one's emotions and on daily events, to adapt to changing situations, and to engage in leisure and fun

- **Social and Cultural**—The ability to work with others, to develop and sustain friendships through cooperation, empathy, negotiation, and take responsibility for one's own actions; the knowledge and motivation to respect differences among individuals of different cultural and economic backgrounds

- **Cognitive and Creative**—A broad base of knowledge and an ability to appreciate and demonstrate creative expression; the ability to see different points of view, integrate ideas, and reflect; good oral, written, problem-solving [skills], and an ability to learn

- **Academic**—The ability and motivation to remain and learn in school through graduation; the ability to study, write, and engage in discussion, and to conduct independent study

- **Vocational**—A broad understanding and awareness of life options and the steps to take in making choices; practical organizational skills, such as time management, budgeting, dealing with systems and bureaucracies. (Zeldin, 1993, p. 10)

Juvenile Justice and Delinquency Prevention (the OJJDP, of the U.S. Department of Justice)—which serves mostly at-risk youth and youth in trouble with the law—the report clearly concurred with Pittman and Wright's description of what youth need.

These two descriptions of needs, from developmental researchers on the one hand and practitioners working with youth on the other, suggest that there is convergence of opinion about the general needs of youth and about the special needs of disadvantaged young people. High/Scope's programmatic response to these needs is to provide a student-centered instructional model based on choice, active participation, plan-do-review, cooperative learning, and leadership, which is embedded in a program framework offering consistent adult support, clear expectations, participatory government, flexible yet carefully designed schedules, emotional and physical safety, plentiful resources, and exposure to new experiences.

The High/Scope Institute for IDEAS offers talented disadvantaged young people both an environment and specific programming that will support their development in appropriate ways. The lessons learned and experience gained in such an environment can offer insights and programming ideas to educators and parents working in a variety of settings.

Endnote

[1] These needs are based on Lefstein and Lipsitz (1986), who in turn based their thinking on Dorman's (1981) work on the Middle Grades Assessment Program.

3

Creating a Supportive Context for Learning

At the High/Scope Institute for IDEAS, each aspect of the program and setting is carefully designed to invite young people to be active learners and to promote group cohesion as well as individual initiative. As Pittman and Wright (1991) stated, "If the role of positive youth development agents is not only to support the development of competencies . . . but also to help youth develop strong positive self-perceptions . . . then positive youth development agents should focus as much on the nature of the *environment* as they do on the *content*" (p. 24).

The learning *context* created for young people can become part of the learning *content*. An appropriate context can teach them how to schedule and use time effectively. It can help them to develop positive attitudes and expectations regarding themselves and others and to organize people and resources for greater engagement. A context that allows them to appreciate and recognize psychological safety can help them to see adults as warm, helpful allies rather than distant authority-figures.

Moreover, the context, or form, of learning can be as important as the content. Young people—and adults as well—often have difficulty with formlessness and lack of direction. But when they are given a flexible structure, one that can be used and adapted to their own goals and purposes and that also offers limits to keep them from getting bogged down, young people often develop a sense of freedom and responsibility. This kind of freedom-giving structure can be termed an *open framework*.

The open framework provides schedules, expectations, guidelines, and limits, which High/Scope staff are trained to work with as a dynamic resource. As staff plan activities, choose arrangements of time or people, and adapt this framework to each specific group of students, the learning context is fleshed out and given life.

In this chapter, the High/Scope open framework is described both as it is presented to new staff who are learning its parameters and also as it looks in practice. Elements of the framework may sound familiar—in ways it resembles a summer camp, and in other ways, a residential school. But what makes it different from both is an attitude that forms quickly in both staff and participants: a sense that they are consciously creating a community, consciously making the Institute experience happen, and using the schedule and resources to enable their plans to be realized. The program belongs to the participants.

It is inspiring to see High/Scope teenagers excited about planning their time and participating in the creation of a learning environment, especially since many have spent their academic life avoiding the requirements of what they consider "the establishment." It is also rewarding to watch young people struggling to define and come to consensus on rules, to understand the purposes of their agreed-upon limitations, and to take themselves and this evolving community seriously.

The Program Schedule

Throughout its month-long session, the Institute for IDEAS schedules a variety of program elements: both staff-initiated and student-initiated activities; individual as well as whole-group endeavors; work and service projects; explorations and investigations; presentations and sharing; quiet reflection and physical activity. The duration and intensity of some of these elements increases as the month progresses. This facilitates greater depth and commitment on the part of students and offers guidance to staff on how to build toward greater engagement and community cohesion.

The Institute's *daily routine* provides consistency and predictability—both of which enable students to "know what is going on" yet take responsibility for planning their use of time and making events happen.

Figure 3.1 outlines the daily routine, showing how it correlates with the developmental needs of adolescents (identified on p. 42 of Chapter 2).

Although such a detailed routine initially might seem regimented, it allows students to think about how to use their time and focus their energy. In addition, the flexibility *within* many of the segments of the routine allows for individual creativity. Room group discussions as well as informal and self-scheduled times enable students to use the daily routine as a tool to find ways to be active and yet pace their activities in a realistic way.

Some students, feeling that they are too busy at the Institute, complain that they do not have enough time to get everything done. However, the fairly rigorous pace of activities and highly scheduled time, when coupled with flexibility and understanding on the part of the staff and directors, can offer students a solid basis for active participation and engagement.

It is worth taking a closer look at the daily routine to see how each program element invites students to action, provides them with exposure to new things, and helps them pace their energies. Throughout the remainder of this chapter, the experiences of three different participants—Anthony, Cynthia, and Jemiel—are related to illustrate how they use and respond to the structure provided by the daily routine.

Elements of the Daily Routine

Rising

Rising time is signaled by a wake-up bell. Students and staff then have 45 minutes to wash, dress, and start the day. Since participants and staff are housed in two buildings (one for boys and one for girls) and live in room groups of four to six students plus a staff member, this part of the day becomes a time to share facilities, to accommodate to others' living patterns, and to learn more about one's own

LEARNING COMES TO LIFE

FIGURE 3.1

THE DAILY ROUTINE: MEETING DEVELOPMENTAL NEEDS

Segments of the Daily Routine	Developmental Needs of Adolescents		
	Diversity of Experiences	Self-Exploration and Definition	Meaningful Participation
Rising 7:45 a.m.			
Breakfast mess-duty 8:15 a.m.			✓
Breakfast 8:30 a.m.		✓	✓
Work crews 9:00 a.m.	✓		✓
Room time 9:35 a.m.	✓		✓
Morning program 10:00 a.m.	✓	(✓)	✓
Informal time 12:00 noon	✓	✓	
Lunch mess-duty 12:15 p.m.			✓
Lunch 12:30 p.m.		✓	✓
Siesta 1:30 p.m.		✓	
Afternoon program 2:30 p.m.	✓	(✓)	✓
Sports 4:05 p.m.			
Dinner mess-duty 5:30 p.m.			✓
Dinner 5:45 p.m.		✓	✓
Self-scheduled time 6:45 p.m.		✓	✓
Evening program 8:00 p.m.	✓	(✓)	✓
Lights out 10:00 p.m.		✓	✓

Note. Parentheses indicate that the time segment *sometimes* involves activities that meet the developmental need.

style of "family" interaction. For the students, many of whom are away from home for the first time, their actions and reactions at this

Positive Interaction With Peers and Adults	Physical Activity	Competence and Achievment	Structure and Limits
✓			✓
✓	(✓)	✓	✓
✓			✓
✓	✓	✓	✓
✓		✓	✓
✓	(✓)	✓	✓
✓	(✓)		
✓	(✓)	✓	✓
✓			✓
			✓
✓	(✓)	✓	✓
✓	✓		✓
✓	(✓)	✓	✓
✓			✓
✓	(✓)	✓	✓
✓	(✓)	✓	✓
✓			✓

time of day can offer valuable insights into their family and home situations. Staff, with planning and effort, are often able to help students use these insights to find more positive ways to live comfortably and respectfully in groups. The following paragraphs describe experiences at rising time for Anthony, Cynthia, and Jemiel:

• • •

Anthony, the oldest of six children, is used to living in cramped quarters (three rooms) with his family. His understanding of how to start the day is to grab what you can. He rushes for the showers ahead of the others, tries to push others out of the way when he wants access to a mirror or sink, and generally tries to be as loud as possible, to make himself heard above the mayhem he expects to be confronted with at the start of each day.

The students in his room group are taken aback by this behavior and complain to the room counselor. The counselor suggests they initiate a talk about what it's like back home first thing in the morning and how they might like to see mornings go differently this month at the Institute. Anthony is amazed to realize that his behavior is unusual. He ends up proposing a series of solutions, starting with his rising quietly 15 minutes earlier, so he won't have to compete with others. Eventually he proposes a rotation system for use of the showers and mirrors, which seems to please most of the others.

• • •

Cynthia, on the other hand, is an only child who is being raised by elderly grandparents. She is greatly put off by the friendly noise and jostling. On several days she has trouble getting out of bed and tells her room group that she is sick and can't come to breakfast. After a few talks with her room counselor, she decides that what she needs to do is get up a bit earlier and do some exercises before breakfast. Her counselor reminds her that she needs to stay in the room until the bell rings, but that as long as she is quiet, she is welcome to do some stretching and other warm-ups in the room while the others are still sleeping. By the third week Cynthia has influenced several girls in her room, and soon four students wake up early and sit together on the floor, taking turns leading stretches before the wake-up bell.

• • •

Jemiel has been termed a "space cadet" by his room group. Twice in the first week he set out for breakfast with mismatching clothes and mismatch-

ing shoes! He claims that back home he can't get going without three cups of coffee. Since everyone has agreed to give up coffee (along with cigarettes and alcohol) for the duration of the Institute, his room group decides to take turns "inspecting" Jemiel before letting him loose on the world. He is good-natured about this, and in helping to take care of Jemiel, the room group develops a nice spirit of camaraderie.

• • •

Breakfast

Breakfast begins at 8:30. Students are assigned to specific table groups for an entire week at a time. These groups, designed to promote interaction and integration of the students, are mixed in gender, cultural background, age, and personality style. Each group not only shares three meals a day together but one day a week shares mess duty (setting up tables before the meals, cleaning tables and floors, and washing dishes afterward). The various groups generally each develop a unique personality, with group members forging their own ways of working and conversing together.

Family-style meals provide students with opportunities to practice sharing, making conversation, being aware of others' needs, and getting along with others.

At each of the meals, a camper-of-the-day (COD), who is invited by a staff member to take on this role, acts as a facilitator in the dining hall. The COD solicits announcements, invites reports or presentations, and leads the group in a recall of what is ahead in the day's schedule. At breakfast, the COD reviews the morning schedule.

Each table also designates a "hopper" to bring food to the table and later clear dishes. Each table group also decides on a week-long system for designating its hopper for each meal, sharing this task equitably.

How Jemiel, Cynthia, and Anthony experience breakfast time is described in the following paragraphs:

• • •

*There is little to say about **Jemiel** at breakfast. He is in such a fog that conversation tends to flow around him. His table group has learned to solicit his opinion from time to time, just to help him come into focus. It is not until the fourth week of the program, however, that Jemiel finally comes to life a bit more for breakfast. He has joined a morning calisthenics group in his house and is a bit more alert. He actually volunteers to be the camper-of-the-day, something that would have been out of the question for him earlier in the session.*

• • •

***Cynthia** is quiet at meals, and Lamantua, one of her table mates, who has also joined her in early morning stretching, is solicitous of her. She asks her opinion, makes sure she is passed the dishes she would like, and generally makes efforts to draw her out. Staff members, also aware of Cynthia's shyness, make an extra effort when sitting with her (staff rotate daily from table to table) to make sure that three boisterous table mates don't overwhelm her or crowd her out of conversations.*

• • •

***Anthony** appears anxious at the first several meals, keeping his eye on the plate as it is passed family-style around the table. He tries to volunteer to be hopper at every meal! The staff member at his table has noticed he's tense and asks him about it, but Anthony denies anything is wrong. Twice, however, he has been unable to eat, because of stomachaches.*

In a discussion at a staff meeting, the director shares the fact that Anthony's family has mentioned on the application form that they have frequently been on food stamps and welfare. Both parents have struggled with chronic unemployment. The staff decides to address Anthony's apparent fear of not getting enough food by letting students know which foods are avail-

able on a regular basis: Regardless of the day's menu, cereal (at breakfast) and peanut butter and jelly sandwiches (at lunch and dinner) will always be available without limit. This general announcement seems to help Anthony tremendously. He eats massive quantities in the first week or two, but has no more difficulties with stomachaches.

• • •

Work Crews

Immediately following breakfast, the community breaks into room groups to carry out small cleaning tasks that require daily attention. Though some participants start out viewing it as drudgery or goof-off time, this work crew time offers several learning possibilities for participants. Most soon realize that they can gain satisfaction from cleaning up after themselves and taking care of the facility; the

Cleaning up after themselves and taking care of the dining facility helps to make students aware of their responsibilities as members of a working community.

place belongs to them more fully while they are there, and the cleanup efforts make them aware of their responsibility to one another.

Participants plan together how to undertake each task and how to divide the labor fairly. The room counselor is a working member of the team, not its leader. Some students have had no experience with doing chores, cleaning, or being responsible for their own environment. Others have carried the whole burden for their family and need to learn how to share tasks with others and delegate responsibilities. Few have had the opportunity to work alongside an adult who is neither an uninvolved overseer nor a "take charge" person who does all the work.

Some examples of work crew tasks are cleaning the girls' or boys' house, checking the grounds for trash, maintaining the garden, and cleaning the dance floor and workshop areas.

The work crew time experiences of Cynthia and Jemiel are described below:

• • •

Having a grandmother who comes home exhausted after a day at work has meant that **Cynthia** *has always done a lot of house cleaning. Once her room group discovers that she has experience with cleaning, they use her as a work crew consultant, asking her to help them compile the list of cleaning tasks that need attention. She also becomes the group's foreman, who apportions tasks according to individual requests and inspects the results. Thus, work crew time becomes a natural opportunity for Cynthia to take on leadership—something she is generally loath to do.*

• • •

Jemiel *is willing to work, or appear to work, but seems to have no sense of how to adequately complete a task. He will sweep a floor, but afterward it looks just as dirty as it did before he started. He is easily distracted, and others in his room group alternate between becoming distracted along with him or becoming annoyed at him for not pulling his weight. The counselor asks him what might help him work more effectively. He shrugs, saying he is not particularly interested in work. Then another group member proposes a contest to see who can pick up the most trash (they are on grounds cleanup that week). This captures Jemiel's attention for a few days.*

The following week, Jemiel is again a halfhearted participant. The group decides to assign him the most concrete tasks, such as taking out the trash and replenishing the toilet paper in the bathrooms. He agrees that it will be better if he can see definite results of his actions.

• • •

Room Time

The room groups function as a small family within the larger community of the Institute. They offer participants an opportunity to form strong bonds, share personal insights and information about themselves, and practice living and interacting with others on a regular basis. Although room groups are mixed in age, race, and cultural background, members of a room group are all of the same gender. This offers students a haven from the pressures of boy-girl dynamics.

In many residential programs, the time participants spend outside certain designated "instruction" times is considered to be "free time," with no special purpose. At the Institute, staff members are trained to consider the program's noninstructional times as important opportunities for helping participants to focus on community building, relating to others individually and in small groups, and using leisure time consciously and purposefully.

Each morning a special time is set aside for room group activities. The room group collectively decides how to spend this time. The only guideline is that the group must stay together. It is common for room groups to go canoeing, to work on projects in the art or shop area, to keep individual journals and then share insights, to go on walks, to have discussions, or to learn songs together.

Staff members, who are always present for these activities, sometimes facilitate the planning process, especially in the early days of the Institute session. But their primary role is to participate, to give students an opportunity to experience adults as companions, not just authority figures.

Room group activities often spawn other student-initiated projects and spill over into other segments of the daily routine. For example, poems that are written as a result of a room group activity might be organized into a dramatic presentation for an evening *musicale* (an evening of performances by students). A group discussion might result in an activity for self-scheduled time, or it might become the basis for a *council* (a reflective evening program in which the whole group gathers around a fire and explores a given theme). A batik project in the art area may lead to a series of meetings at which students design and make special shirts to wear for folk dancing.

This group chooses to spend their "room time" at the canoe pond. This noninstructional time lets them focus on community building, relating to one another, and using leisure time purposefully.

The following accounts show what room group time leads to for Jemiel, Anthony, and Cynthia:

• • •

*Although **Jemiel** has never been canoeing before, after trying it for the first time, he is hooked. He wants to go canoeing every day, but after a while this bores some room group members who would rather spend room time learning how to use the tools in the shop area. After much heated discussion, Jemiel reluctantly agrees to accompany his room group to the shop area.*

Once there, however, he becomes engrossed in making a model canoe that will float. Toward the end of the week, he talks to one of the workshop counselors about the possibility of repairing an old pontoon raft he has found behind the barn. The counselor, Ben, agrees to think about it and requests some books from the library on raft building. Two days later, Jemiel and two other students meet after dinner with Ben to plan a raft-repair project that evolves into a workshop to explore "floatables" and to create model boats that float.

• • •

***Anthony** wants his room group to play basketball every free moment. However, two members of the room group have literary interests and hate basketball. When they agree to try it once, the experience is a disaster. Anthony feels held back by the nonplayers, and the nonplayers feel intimidated in a game of basketball, even when it is played with High/Scope's noncompetitive-style rules.*

Anthony agrees that basketball is not a great idea for this particular group but confesses it is how he spends all his free time at home. The group decides to read together the novel Of Mice and Men. *To his surprise, Anthony discovers he enjoys it. After a few days of reading, they decide to prepare a dramatic production of Steinbeck's novel to perform later in the session. They assign the dramatic roles to members of their room group but invite others to participate in the production by making scenery and props and preparing costumes.*

• • •

Cynthia's *room group decides to explore working with clay. After an initial session in which they each make circles with their initials in them, the counselor suggests they get a little wild and creative. They decide to make their own beads for a large three-dimensional bead mosaic to hang in the dining room. It eventually evolves into an activity that is open to the whole Institute community, and several students use their self-scheduled time to complete it.*

This room group agrees at the end of the month that half the pleasure of their room group experience has been the great discussions that sprang up while they were making the beads and designing the wall hanging. Although Cynthia was usually quiet during these discussions, she says she feels closer to these girls than she's ever felt to anyone before in her life.

• • •

Morning Program

Students spend most of their morning in small groups engaged in instructional, exploratory programs called *work projects* (explained on p. 78 of this chapter) and *workshops* or *clubs* (explained on p. 74 of this chapter). The calendar on pp. 90–91 shows a typical distribution of clubs, workshops, and work projects throughout the month-long session. Workshops and clubs, which are instructional activities led by individual staff members (sometimes by pairs of staff), offer interdisciplinary hands-on experience with the arts and sciences. Participants are first given a short description of each activity and then asked to list their first three choices. The selections that follow describe the workshops chosen by Jemiel, Anthony, and Cynthia.

Jemiel has chosen the Floatables workshop, which he helped to plan. Ben, the workshop counselor, is aware that he will need to help Jemiel harness his energy. Without such help, Jemiel has the potential to either dominate a group or distract it. Jemiel is one of the most skilled with the tools, so Ben asks him to pair up with other members of the workshop, to help them get "certified" on the power tools they will need to use for the job. The planning session goes very well. Jemiel puts his energy into asking the group questions rather than dominating with his opinions. He ends up stimulating some great brainstorming.

• • •

Anthony wants to do mask-making, which surprises the staff at first. When the director talks with him about his choice, he replies: "Masks are from Africa; that's my thing." The director alerts Maria, the counselor, to Anthony's expectation, and Maria makes sure that several examples from Africa, as well as from other parts of the world, are among the masks available at the workshop.

Anthony has trouble staying interested in the group process. He doesn't want to discuss masks from other cultures. He keeps saying, "All the important masks are from Africa." Ernesto, a student of Mexican heritage, challenges that statement, and Anthony threatens to beat him up, at which point Maria intervenes.

She asks each of them to look at masks from their respective cultures and to figure out what makes them powerful or interesting. The students break into two subgroups to consider this question and to help Anthony and Ernesto list the characteristics of the masks from their respective cultures. Upon reconvening to share their results, the groups discover that their two lists are similar.

Anthony agrees, finally, that he was being stubborn because his art teacher at school did not believe African art was important. Each group then decides to create two masks apiece—one showing their heritage and the other showing their present or future culture. Anthony gradually gets interested in the other students' pieces, and he seems to enjoy the challenge of creating his own.

• • •

Cynthia chooses a paper-making workshop, and as in most activities, she's a quiet but willing participant. As the week evolves, it becomes apparent *that Cynthia has quite a bit of artistic talent. She begins to vary the materi-als she puts into her paper, and the other students take an interest in what she is doing, wandering over to watch and ask questions.*

Andrea, the counselor, picks up on these interactions and invites Cynthia to lead a brainstorming session on what variations the group would like to try—both individually and collectively. Cynthia is pleased with this task, and her peers are enthusiastic about the paper she has cre-ated. They ask her to lead their group presentation in the dining hall after dinner. At first she hesitates, but after being encouraged by a particularly outgoing peer, she agrees to try.

Staff members note later that Cynthia is quietly developing an effec-tive leadership style. Although her style is different from some of the more flamboyant, extroverted leaders, her peers have gradually grown to respect her, and she is blossoming in response to their interest in her.

• • •

Based on students' workshop preferences, the Institute di-rectors make individual assignments, ensuring not only that student choices are honored but also that groups are balanced and manageable for staff.

Informal Time

The time segment between the morning program and lunch serves as a respite dur-ing which participants are free to read, write letters, work on individual projects, min-gle with others, play with Frisbees, or work at computers.

Informal time serves as a respite. Students are free to read, write letters, work on individual projects, mingle with others, or finish up workshop or club activities.

Informal time is the only segment of the daily routine when participants are not expected to schedule or account for their activity.

As the Institute session progresses, however, students often do use some of their informal time to work on the overflow of their activities—to finish up projects in the art room or shop, to practice plays, or to reconvene with room groups, for example.

Staff members remain involved during this time to circulate, to be available as resources, to talk with students who need to think something through, and to make sure that all students are present and accounted for.

Lunch

The midday meal is generally more lively than breakfast. It is a time for table groups to check in with one another and report on the morning's events. The midday and evening meals are good times for students to practice their skills in conversation, in being aware of the needs of others, in sharing, and in getting along with others.

While at the Institute, students build up an impressive repertoire of songs from around the globe. Shared group experiences like singing and folk dancing are important in building a sense of community at the Institute.

After the meal there is a time for singing. Over the month-long session, the students are able to build an impressive repertoire of songs from around the globe. Some participants are immediately enthusiastic about the group singing; others are a bit reluctant. Staff members are trained, however, to teach songs in a nonintimidating way that generally draws all the students into the activity, creating a wonderful sense of community and success. Because the songs are usually ballads, rounds, or folk songs that offer a chance to create new verses, they are especially conducive to group participation.

After singing, there is time for workshop or work project groups to offer a short presentation of their progress. This enables everyone to have a good sense of what others are doing, and it gives students an opportunity to speak before peers in an organized fashion. Students feel invested and engaged, both in what they are doing and in what their peers are doing.

Siesta

After lunch, a period of time is set aside for resting and reflecting. Students have the option of resting on their beds or spending their siesta time at different locations around the Institute grounds, in a variety of quiet activities.

During siesta, students are asked to remain at least 20 feet apart from one another, girls and boys stay on their respective sides of the grounds, and everyone remains quiet, not communicating with others. This is a time for students to write letters home, to read books, to write poetry, and to reflect on their activities.

Afternoon Program

The afternoon program is similar to the morning program; it usually involves a staff-designed, student-centered, small-group activity—normally a club, workshop, or work project. Jemiel's experience with afternoon program time is described here:

Having time alone to write, to read, to reflect on the day's events, is important. During siesta, students remain quiet and are asked not to communicate with others.

• • •

Jemiel finds it difficult to get going during the afternoon program, as do several others. In his case, he feels sleepy and has trouble staying focused on what he is doing. Instead, he tends to cut up, to make jokes and clown around.

His room counselor, who also happens to be facilitating the work project he is part of (to divert water from a brook to irrigate an organic garden that the group is going to plant), takes him aside to talk for a few minutes.

When asked, Jemiel doesn't know why he is cracking so many jokes. "Maybe I need more time to hang out," he suggests.

"When you get that time back home, do you tend to joke around less?" the staff member asks.

Jemiel admits that it doesn't seem to make any difference. Finally after more discussion, Jemiel comes to the conclusion that he is bored with the planning stage; he wants to get to the action. The counselor asks if Jemiel might be interested in videotaping the planning discussion, as part of a representation of the whole process to be shown to the entire Institute group later in the session. Liking that idea, Jemiel runs to the office to get the video camera. When he returns, the group spends a few minutes discussing with him what kinds of things he might need to capture on tape. He then experiments a bit with the equipment, and the planning session continues—this time with Jemiel contributing occasional suggestions or interview questions. He is now thoroughly interested and engaged.

• • •

Sports Time

Each day at this time, participants and staff choose to participate in one of three sports being offered. These include such games as soccer, volleyball, softball, basketball, and "ultimate Frisbee," as well as dance, aerobics, and jogging. The three sports offered each day are chosen to provide a variety of activity levels. Although not everyone is interested in sports, each student is expected to engage in some kind of physical activity. Most eventually discover that when games are played cooperatively rather than competitively and when activities are designed to embrace all levels of ability, sports can be quite enjoyable.

Many participants have never played team sports like soccer or volleyball; others are used to playing these games at a highly competitive level. At High/Scope the rules of these games are modified, often by each group of students, to be more inclusive and cooperative. The goal is to reduce the intimidation suffered by beginners and by less coordinated participants, while providing skilled players with opportunities to channel their abilities into working as team members. The more skilled players are encouraged to take the lead in assisting others in developing their skills.

For example, in soccer, the emphasis is on playing a position and passing the ball. In volleyball, the emphasis is on setting up the ball to teammates and maintaining the volley. In basketball, each member of a team must handle the ball before a basket is considered valid. In all sports, *encouragement* is the rule. The following paragraphs describe how the High/Scope approach works for Cynthia and for Anthony:

• • •

One goal of sports at High/Scope is to reduce the intimidation typically suffered by beginners and less coordinated students. Noncompetitive sports allow students with varying ability levels to participate together and have fun.

Cynthia does not generally like sports. She is heavyset and in the past has experienced being teased by others and being chosen last for teams. For the first week or so, she has taken part only in sports activities that seem safe or individual, such as jogging or aerobics. However, halfway into the second week, her room group decides, through consensus, to all go to volleyball together.

Although she doesn't speak up to object, this prospect terrifies Cynthia. She feels tense about it all morning and ends up in tears on her bed during siesta time. When room group members ask her what is wrong, she first says she is sick. But with a bit more prodding, she admits that she hates sports and doesn't want to go to volleyball. Sonji perseveres in asking her why and finally elicits what Cynthia is afraid of. The group agrees to support Cynthia and to see if there's some way to make it fun for her.

After several minutes of stretching in the barn with the entire Institute group, Cynthia's group heads out to the volleyball field. They inform the others who arrive that today they want to play together as a team, and they suggest 20 minutes of drill, in which the object is to throw the ball directly to someone on the other team instead of trying to make the other team miss the ball. So everyone can experience success at serving, they institute a serving policy wherein the "first good ball in" will count.

It takes Cynthia several days to get over her aversion to volleyball. But she confesses that it "isn't that bad." Sometime in the third week, she actually joins a volleyball game at informal time. Although she doesn't have much accuracy yet, she does hit the ball with a lot of power. The others all encourage her in this and congratulate her on her powerful serves.

• • •

*For **Anthony**, "sports" mean basketball. His first instinct is to check out "who can play" and to try to organize a "real game." When he hears about the High/Scope approach of multilevel participation, a look of disgust comes over his face. For several days he struggles with the new rules, trying to focus on team play and helping the less skilled players. But he complains bitterly about not having any fun, which results in one sports time when only the skilled players show up to play. As they begin falling into their usual patterns of "real ball," the staff member playing with them intervenes. She points out that their style of highly competitive play will prevent others from trying the game. They argue that only highly competitive players have shown up today, and so it's okay.*

She suggests they come up with a drill or new rule that will challenge their skill but not create such fierce competition. She explains that her goal is not to teach them that competition is wrong, but rather to give them an alternative experience that they wouldn't get back home. Agreeing to discuss the whole topic of sports at the community meeting, they decide to work on passing and dribbling drills for the rest of the hour.

Anthony, angry and frustrated, slams around for a while. The others avoid him at first, but at dinner one of his closer friends leans over and whispers in his ear to "knock it off." He isn't able to get rid of his mood, so after dinner the counselor who intervened in the game goes for a walk with him and invites him to come up with a form of basketball that will work for him, while still honoring the spirit of cooperation that High/Scope stands for.

Anthony agrees to this challenge but ends up playing other sports for the rest of the session. He doesn't seem to have the same problem with foregoing competition in sports that he does not regularly play back home. Another group does manage to come up with some satisfactory basketball rules that work for most of the young people. Anthony occasionally agrees to act as a coach, but for the most part he is unable to let go of his resentment that "real rules" won't be followed.

Instead of engaging in a battle with him over basketball rules, staff members decide to encourage Anthony to keep trying other sports. He understands the reasoning behind the limitation but is not ready to accept it. Late in the session he develops a real passion for soccer. He turns out to be a very capable and considerate team player in that context, so staff members encourage him to think about how to transfer to the basketball court the enjoyment he gets in soccer. He agrees to think about it.

• • •

Informal Time

This 45-minute block, like morning informal time, provides a recreative break before supper. Swimming is an option during this time. All swimmers use the buddy system, and a certified lifeguard is always on duty. Students who do not swim are free to do what they want, within the immediate area of the houses and barn. During informal times at the Institute, as well as during other activities and projects, the forming of exclusive friendships or romantic couples is discouraged. The account that follows illustrates the difficulties that such pairings can create:

• • •

Jemiel fell in love with Melindy on the second day of the Institute. On the fourth day Melindy fell in love with Jemiel, and they became an "item" in everyone's eyes. This stimulated some competition among members of their respective room groups, who felt that they too should have a girlfriend or boyfriend. Jemiel and Melindy were pretty careful not to be too demonstrative, because they were aware of the Institute policy that couples are only acceptable if they are inclusive *rather than* exclusive *of others.*

The tension culminated early though, when toward the end of the first week, Jemiel and Melindy disappeared during an informal time. The staff, aware of the potential danger of allowing this couple to "sneak off" and thus set a precedent for others, sent a couple of staff members, Ben and Sarah, to find them.

Jemiel and Melindy were offended to have their privacy breached— they were only talking and kissing after all. Ben, who found them sitting alone in the maze field, explained that he did not want to interfere with their getting close, but that staff wanted to make sure that their relationship remained a constructive one during the next three weeks. He pointed out that being exclusive causes students to miss out on friendships with the rest of the community and on program opportunities. He invited them to continue their private conversation on the side lawn, where they would be in view of others, but not to set a bad example for other couples, who might then feel pressured to sneak off together.

That night, the staff initiated discussions in the boys' and girls' houses about couples and about students' feelings regarding the Institute's policies. Several students agreed with the policy of discouraging romantic couples, saying it made them feel less pressure about their sexual status. Individuals who were already seen as part of a couple felt for the most part that there wasn't enough time to get to know another person well. Most of them, however, could see the wisdom of taking advantage of the many choices provided by the program rather than getting "lost" in one other person.

These impromptu meetings were just the beginning of what turned out to be a series of discussions about relationships, sex and gender issues, feelings, and what it means to get to know another person.

In not avoiding the topic altogether but setting some limits on how students could express their sexual energies and feelings, staff stimulated students to think about what they want for themselves and from each other and to question some of the prevalent attitudes about sex—attitudes they encounter back home and in their schools. The Institute's goal is to provide a safe environment, inclusive of everyone, but exclusive of behaviors that create factions or cliques within the community. Because this goal is clear and consistent, most students accept the limitations as reasonable though perhaps annoying. They accept the challenge to get to know one another creatively through *rather than* apart from *the program.*

Jemiel and Melindy cooled off toward each other by the end of the third week. Their breakup was not too problematic, however. Jemiel moped around for a day, and Melindy became very involved in a building project during her informal time. The other students were able to be supportive of the breakup without needing to take sides.

• • •

Dinner

The evening meal tends to be a relaxed time; students have an opportunity to share the events of the day with those at their table. Dinner is again followed by singing, reports or presentations from the afternoon program, and announcements.

Self-Scheduled Time (SST)

Self-scheduled time, which begins after dinner and ends at approximately 8:00 p.m., is similar to informal time in that participants choose where to be and what activity to engage in. However, during SST, students choose from a variety of activities offered by either staff or their peers. This segment gives students an opportunity to teach one another new skills, to organize group projects, to continue activities from workshops or clubs in the company of others, and to follow through on ideas by planning together with others.

Students often use their self-scheduled time to achieve closure on a project, to work on a drama or rehearse for musicale, or to practice a skill that is necessary to a workshop or project activity (but too time-consuming for them to master within the afternoon segment). Typical SST activities include poetry reading, sketching in the art area, practicing on the potter's wheel, working on the Institute's newspaper, repairing a small engine, discussing current events, engaging in creative writing, working on computers, and developing pictures in the photo lab.

The staff member in charge of the evening's announcements makes sure that a variety of SST activities are available each day. Staff members see to it that each student is focused on some activity, since many young people find their energy waning at this time of day.

Evening Program

Each night at approximately 8:00 p.m., the entire Institute community gathers for the evening program, which involves the active participation of all members. This is a chance for students to see and feel the power of their combined talents and personalities and to experience the growing comfort and satisfaction that arise as the community identity takes shape. The evening program, like so many Institute activities, often brings out undiscovered talents, as is illustrated by this account of Anthony's part in an evening program:

• • •

Anthony failed math at school this year for a second time. He has told his room group all about it—how stupid and meaningless the subject seems to him. But for one evening program, the Institute group splits up into smaller groups (chosen in this instance by the director, who wants each group to have a good mix of ages and ability levels), and each group is given a quantity to measure. One group is asked to figure out how many stones are in the gravel driveway in front of the brick house; another is asked to determine how many blades of grass make up the side lawn; yet another group is asked to figure out how much water is in the pond. Anthony's group is asked to determine how much dirty laundry is in the 25 bags sitting on the front porch, waiting to be taken to the laundromat the next morning.

Anthony at first grumbles about the task, assuming they must somehow count each smelly item. But then one group member points out that they can find a way to estimate it. There is much discussion back and forth about how to measure without actually emptying the bags. Anthony, for some reason, gets absorbed in the problem and comes up with several valuable suggestions.

After calculating for about half an hour, the groups reconvene in the barn to present their findings. Each group discusses the process they followed to arrive at their conclusions. Anthony volunteers to do the presentation for his group. Later he mentions to his room group how much he enjoyed the evening program. They all start laughing. When he asks, "What is the joke?" they point out that he has just spent an entire evening doing math.

• • •

Evening program activities, which vary widely in content, range from folk dancing and original drama performances to the investigation of mathematical systems. Students are given an opportunity to be exposed to a variety of ideas and fields and to broaden their horizons in an enjoyable, relaxed context. "Successful Evening Programs" on pp. 70–72 describes typical evening activities.

Evening programs provide participants with the opportunity to create and implement ideas, to work cooperatively with others in various-sized groups, and to explore new realms. Often programs stimulate thoughts and conversations that are pursued by students and staff in their room group and bedtime conversations.

Lights Out

Following the evening program, participants and staff return to their rooms together and get ready for bed. The time spent in the rooms following lights out is an important part of the day because it allows time for individuals to reflect on their feelings about the day and about the Institute in general. Students use the time to talk about serious social issues and to share aspects of their personal lives and backgrounds.

For some students it is the first time they have had a view into how other people live—what their families are like, what stresses they cope with beneath their "cool" exteriors, what they want or dream about. It is also new for them to have discussions in "mixed" groups—with people from diverse backgrounds, ages, and ethnic identities.

Staff and students often read stories or poems by flashlight, sing quiet songs, or share journal entries before going to bed. Not all the room groups are instantly harmonious or successful—individuals have to work hard to understand one another, to find ways of living harmoniously, to respect differences in style, and to have constructive conversations rather than critical or destructive ones.

This part of the evening is when important breakthroughs often happen—when a young person feels safe to mention something in the dark, with an intimate group, that he or she wouldn't feel comfortable bringing up in the light of day, with a broader group. It is a time when the relaxed, caring mood that lingers over

SUCCESSFUL EVENING PROGRAMS

FOLK DANCE
A folk dance instructor taught the group different cultural dances to perform together. She worked on specific balance and coordination skills, progressing to more and more complex dances throughout the month of the Institute.

EGG DROP
In this popular evening program, participants met in small groups and were given one bag of materials, which they then were to use to construct a vehicle that would protect an egg when dropped from a 20-foot balcony onto the ground below. Groups came up with various means of protecting their eggs—parachutes, suspension structures, protective padding. Groups gathered at the end of the program to see which eggs survived the fall.

SCIENCE SKITS
Institute participants divided into small groups, each including one staff member. Every group was given two topics: a specific simple machine (such as a washing machine or telescope) and a specific scientific process (such as mitosis or the water cycle). The groups then wrote silent skits to represent the given topics and performed the skits. The audience tried to guess what topics were being portrayed.

MUSICALE
The evening was organized and introduced by participants. Performances included songs, plays, art projects, and poetry readings created during the Institute session. Certain individuals also presented solo performances that they had developed on their own, prior to or during the Institute session.

GROUP DYNAMICS
Participants were divided evenly into groups, and each member was assigned a role to play during a group discussion on an assigned topic. Roles students were to play included instigator, idea-giver, peacemaker, leader. Not until the end of the evening were group members aware of what roles various persons were playing. The evening ended with a discussion of group dynamics and problem solving.

FRACTURED FAIRY TALES
Several small groups, each made up of students and a staff member, were given traditional fairy tales to modernize in any way they saw fit. The groups then developed skits portraying their modified fairy tales and performed them for the Institute community.

COUNCIL
A topic was presented for participants to contemplate as they quietly walked out through the fields to sit around a fire ring. Popular topics for council discussion were "taking risks," "building trust," and "dealing with peer pressure." As students sat around the fire, any individual could comment on the topic. Everyone's opinion was directed to the fire, and no one conversed directly or challenged anyone's opinion.

COLLEGE NIGHT
After a tour of the University of Michigan campus, the group divided and moved through several stations, where they could ask specific college-related questions of staff members. They were able to discuss choosing a college or university, deciding on a major, obtaining financial aid, participating in athletics or fraternities and sororities. They also could discuss the option of vocational training.

PARTICIPANT-LED EVENING PROGRAMS
A small group of participants learned the difficulties of controlling the large group by leading the Institute community in forming "opinion continuums." The leaders would pose such a question as What size of city do you want to live in? Participants were to discuss the question with one another until they could line themselves up according to a continuum of opinions, ranging from those preferring the smallest town to those preferring the biggest city. This format was followed on different topics to generate discussion and consideration of different opinions.

COMMUNICATION/SPATIAL RELATIONS GAME
Participants worked in pairs to sharpen their communication skills. One partner in each pair verbally described a simple geometric drawing to the other, while the listening partner attempted to draw it. The resulting drawing enabled partners to see how effectively they could communicate. This was repeated using three-dimensional objects. One partner arranged the objects while narrating to his or her partner, who then attempted to create an identical arrangement.

GAME OF LIFE
In this future-planning activity, each participant was assigned an identity including a specific age, income, and status (e.g., educational, marital). Each day over the course of three days, participants would submit individual plans that (1) distributed their assigned income to bills, savings, investment, purchases, etc., and (2) helped them change status, for example, by finishing school. New identities assigned the next day would reflect what the students had submitted, either by penalizing participants for mistakes (such as overspending) or rewarding them for accomplishments.

PIPE STACKING
Using aluminum pipes, twine, and parachute material, groups of participants created outdoor sculptures in various shapes. Some symbolized ideas, others expressed feelings. Each group wrote a haiku poem about their sculpture to present to the rest of the Institute community. The sculptures were left standing for the rest of the Institute session.

PREDATOR GAME
Each participant chose an identity on nature's food chain (herbivore, carnivore, omnivore). Based on these identities, individuals then had to hunt or hide from one another, as groups

Continued on next page

scattered around the Institute grounds. If a person was touched by someone who was hunting her or him, then that person was out of the game. Three individuals representing *disease, weather,* and *humans* only had to point to any of the other game participants to put them out of the game.

SPVs (SELF-PROPELLED VEHICLES)

Participants worked in small groups to build self-propelled vehicles. They could use anything they could find in the shop, including wood, string, rubber bands, balloons, paper. Afterwards, each group presented its ideas to the Institute community and demonstrated its vehicle's performance by attempting to propel it across the barn floor.

SPACE DANCING

Small groups of participants were each given a familiar folk song, as well as a specific area of the Institute grounds in which to perform. Each group was asked to choreograph a dance to accompany the song and somehow incorporate the surrounding environment into the performance. After the small groups had practiced, the Institute community traveled together from area to area to watch and listen to each group's performance.

DISEASE-TRANSMISSION SIMULATION GAME

Participants were each given a cup containing water. One person unknowingly received water that contained one drop of acid. Each participant then exchanged some liquid with another participant, recording with whom the exchange was made. This activity was repeated until everyone had made and recorded three exchanges. Then all cups of liquid were tested with PH indicators for acidity. A study followed to figure out who originally had the "contaminated" water and what the probability was of getting "infected" with it. A prediction was also developed based on starting with a different number of "contaminators" and exchanging liquids a different number of times, and the experiment was then repeated to verify the prediction.

INTERNATIONAL CULTURAL FESTIVAL

A group of students worked with a staff member during SST time for a week to plan and prepare for an evening program that would focus on sharing cultural information. They planned with other students, drew maps, made decorations, wrote menus, and organized the logistics of the evening. During the festival, students divided into groups and rotated among various booths and activities that other students presented. At each booth, participants tried a sample of food and participated in a game or activity that taught them something about the culture represented. It was a respectful and festive evening that replaced a lot of myths with real information about people and places.

from evening program helps participants to open up to one another in new ways and to value their differences as well as their common-alities. The following account shows how Cynthia made a break-through during lights out time:

• • •

Cynthia is not much of a talker, but following an evening program about disease transmission, she confesses to her room group after lights out that she is worried about people with AIDS who have no health insurance. She has seen a television show on the topic, and since she and most of her friends are without health insurance, it has caused her to consider the whole situation of people on welfare and people who are uninsured and what they do when dis-aster strikes. Her insights into some of the stresses faced by the uninsured people she knows spark a lively discussion in her room group. Cynthia is surprised by the interest that her roommates take in this topic that she has brought up. It gives her a special sense of belonging that evening.

Instructional Program Elements

At the High/Scope Institute for IDEAS, the instructional program elements are primarily *clubs and workshops, work projects, evening pro-grams, field trips,* and *special workshops.* Each of these forms of activity offers students a different kind of focus, time span, and dimension.

It is useful to note that although students are required to choose, sign up for, and make commitments to specific program choices, they are not locked into a single course of action. Students do not get tracked into specializing in particular subject areas or working at a particular level of expertise. Instead, they always work in mixed-level, mixed-age groupings and are encouraged to explore as wide a variety of subjects as possible.

By not referring to instructional activities as courses or classes, the Institute hopes to overcome any negative preconceptions stu-dents may have about learning or instruction. By offering students new formats for learning and by using a flexible student-centered style of teaching, staff try to change young peoples' attitudes toward learning. Instruction is designed to accommodate a variety of interests. There is no curriculum with prescribed materials to be covered; there is no achievement testing. The curriculum evolves in response to student and staff interests, and the material that is covered is determined by the creativity and enthusiasm of the staff and students together. What students gain or achieve is demonstrated through tangible products, performances, presentations, and student satisfaction. It is amazing to witness the breadth of experience, the depth of understanding, and the level of engagement produced by this open-framework, interdisciplinary style of instruction. Following are brief descriptions and some examples of various forms of program activity.

Clubs and Workshops

Clubs and workshops are small-group instructional activities that allow students to explore a wide variety of topics, such as mathematics, history, science, journalism, photography, and theater. Clubs, which are designed to introduce students to ideas, materials, and methods, are short-term, meeting for only two to four sessions of an hour and three quarters each. Workshops are similar to clubs in form and content but extend for a longer time—about eight to ten sessions—allowing students to explore subjects at greater depth.

Clubs. Clubs, the instructional activities that meet only two to four times, are offered at the beginning of the Institute month as a way to get participants gradually used to the High/Scope approach to active learning instruction. The work sessions of these clubs are staff-planned, offering students a chance to sample a topic and explore new possibilities without requiring overwhelming time and energy commitments from them. The clubs are designed to introduce students to ideas, materials, and methods that they are not likely to discover on their own or in conventional high school classrooms. (See "Examples of Past Clubs.")

Student-led clubs. During each Institute session, students are also encouraged to design and lead some instructional clubs for groups of their peers. Staff become mentors or advisors to interested individuals to help them in planning these sessions. Staff members introduce the student leaders to a variety of teaching techniques:

EXAMPLES OF PAST CLUBS

THE CULTURE CLUB

For this two-session club, the medium was block printing. The first session consisted of some warm-up carving and printing. Students studied, discussed, and created their own interpretations of different styles of African art. They designed their own images, using African motifs, and then carved them into linoleum blocks. The final session was spent combining each person's print onto a large fabric, which was hung in the barn for the remainder of the Institute. The participants described to the rest of the Institute community their product (an "Adinkra" cloth, which is a traditional African wall hanging), the process used to make it, and the African history and significance of the piece.

STORYTELLING

This club began with the staff member doing an expressive reading of a short story to the group. Students then discussed the importance of style, facial expression, intonation, and gestures in terms of public speaking and storytelling. Each participant chose a story to share with the group and took some time to practice telling it aloud. When the group reconvened, each participant shared his or her story and others offered constructive feedback. After this exercise the group sat in a circle and told a group story by passing a "magic rock" around the circle. Each participant added a few sentences to the story. This activity was

very popular and was repeated with the entire group around a campfire.

NEWSCAST

This club began with a discussion about what makes news, what role morals and values play in journalism, and what makes news interesting or exciting. Then students wrote articles about topics that they felt needed exploration at the Institute. These ranged from an interview with each staff member to a research piece about the origins of High/Scope. For several days the group presented a news update to the entire community after lunch. This club later formed the journalism workshop, which produced the community's newspaper.

POTTERY

To introduce the participants to clay, each person was blindfolded and handed a chunk of clay to work with. The group spent several minutes exploring the tactile qualities of the clay, feeling its texture and malleability, experimenting with different shapes, and making "blind sculptures." The group focused on such hand construction-techniques as coil, pinch, and slab. A staff member presented a short demonstration on the potter's wheel. Soon each student was working on a wheel, experimenting with centering clay and throwing pots. Pottery quickly became a very popular activity for informal time and self-scheduled time.

Continued on next page

EXAMPLES OF PAST CLUBS continued

MASKS AND CANDLES

This club began with mask-making. Working in pairs, students each took a turn applying a plaster mask to a partner's face. After the masks dried, they were peeled off and decorated with paint. Making candles required participants to concentrate and use caution in working with hot wax. They heated up the waxes, created bases, attached wicks to them, and then dipped their own candles.

MAY YOUR DREAMS COME TRUE

This club focused on goal *setting* versus goal *achievement*. Students began by discussing their dreams and then moved on to discussing more realistic goals, breaking each down into small tasks and stages. Some participants worked alone, while others paired up and used an interview format to extract from one another the thinking and questions behind stated goals. The group acted out a situation in which they were an advertising agency taking on the task of producing a commercial for a product. The planning stages were key as the group set everyone's long- and short-term goals for accomplishing the task. After the production, they evaluated whether or not the goals had been reached.

BRIDGE BUILDING

This club began with an exploration of various load-bearing structures. Students made models with wood to discover what shapes and designs were most effective in bearing weight. Participants then built their own bridges using balsa wood, toothpicks, and other types of wood. The goal was to create a bridge that could support 40 pounds. Though everyone succeeded in creating a bridge capable of supporting the required weight, the bridges were extremely different in size, materials, and shape. One bridge was even capable of bearing a participant's body weight.

beginning with an active experience, organizing a planning or goal-setting session, and allowing for individualized activities within the larger framework of instruction.

Many students are delighted to find they have something to teach and are pleased to become more familiar with the High/Scope approach to teaching and learning. It makes them more enthusiastic participants and gives them ideas about how to work with their studies more actively back home.

Student-led clubs meet for an hour and a half at a time, usually meeting one to three times. Although staff members attend the club meetings as supportive participants, they are careful not to dominate or take over the experience from the students.

The following is a list of clubs that students circulated to describe what they were offering in a recent year. Some of the topics, such as Fractals, were extensions of experiences students had in staff-led clubs. Others

In workshops, staff challenge students to work with ideas, concepts, and group process in depth, so they are able to create a highly developed product or presentation. Students in this drama workshop rehearsed diligently to prepare for their play.

(such as Fancy Drill) reflect skills that individual students brought with them from home and wished to share.

- **Fractals.** Come to the brick "rec room" and explore computer-generated fractals for yourself.

- **Fancy Drill.** We will meet in the barn to work on this dance/drill technique. Beginners are welcome!

- **Singing.** We will work on some new songs as well as some old ones. We will probably learn some to teach in the dining hall. If you have songs in mind, or just want to sing more, come to this club.

- **Karate.** Come to the karate club to work on beginning karate techniques. Both girls and boys are encouraged to join!

- **Shop/Lathes.** Come to the shop to work on lathe projects. You can make candlesticks, lamp posts, or whatever you wish. Beginners are welcome to come and be certified.

- **Printing.** Work on printing techniques using potatoes. We will carve them, use paint to print with them, and create patterns and designs on paper.

- **Gliders.** Glide right down to the science area for the glider club, where we will be designing and building our own gliders out of balsa wood.

- **Solar Hot Dog Cooking.** Come to this club if you're interested in cooking without the conventions of stove, oven, or fire. Everyone will actually build a solar cooker. This will be useful as a survival skill in the wilderness. Meet in the woodshop.

- **Photograms.** For those who haven't been to the darkroom yet—learn the basics of photo printing and darkroom technique by creating photograms.

Workshops. As with clubs, students who sign up for a workshop commit to attending all meetings of that workshop. This allows them to work with ideas, concepts, and group process in depth and to create a highly developed product or presentation. As with clubs, staff offer descriptions of several workshop choices at one time, so participants can select an activity that truly interests them. The main goal behind workshops is to help participants recognize that they possess all the necessary tools to learn, answer questions, draw conclusions, and address complicated problems on their own.

Staff members usually begin the instructional process of a workshop (and of a club) with an active experience, so participants will become immediately and concretely engaged. Most workshops involve a process to learn, a tangible product to create, an explorational path to follow, a concept to operationalize, a question to answer, or specific tools to master to achieve some goal. These tap into young people's natural motivation and curiosity. When instruction is too abstract or vague, it almost always flounders in this setting—students thrive on being able to ground their explorations in concrete goals, plans, and outcomes.

For an example of the variety of workshops offered at a recent Institute session, see "One Session's Workshop Offerings."

Work Projects

Work projects are multifaceted. They involve physical effort, diverse kinds of problem solving, aesthetic considerations, and group coop-

ONE SESSION'S WORKSHOP OFFERINGS

SCIENCE

This introductory science workshop covered a wide range of topics, beginning with microbiology. Students began by gathering water samples from the pond to observe under the microscope. Next, the group looked at different kinds of engines, discussing how they worked. They also put together an astronomy presentation for the large group; it explained what constellations are visible at a certain time and how to find them. Students in this workshop visited local hands-on and natural science museums, reporting their findings to the rest of the members of the Institute. Participants wrapped up the workshop by talking about genetics, probability, and disease transmission, and they planned and facilitated an evening program on disease transmission.

SPEECHES AND SKITS

This workshop began by exploring three different types of speeches: informative, persuasive, and demonstrative. After working with these speech types, the group decided to write a proposal to make two changes in the Institute daily routine. Later, this group facilitated a meeting at which they presented their proposal to their fellow students and staff. The proposal was voted on, and the changes were approved. The remainder of the workshop was spent working on a series of skits. The participants divided into small groups and each

developed a skit to present to the others. One skit was later expanded and turned into a larger production.

WOODSHOP

This workshop provided students with a basic knowledge of woodworking skills and shop tools. Participants designed and built their own projects, incorporating four common elements: conceptualization, construction, evaluation, and demonstration. Students began by making a two-dimensional representation of their concept, indicating required measurement and materials. Next, they used tools (such as jigsaws, table saws, and drills) and processes (such as lamination, sanding, painting, and varnishing) to construct their project. Finally, students evaluated their work and presented their creations to the rest of the Institute community. Typical projects were making lamps, baseball bats, and model sailboats.

POETRY

The poetry workshop provided students with an opportunity to write and read poetry in an environment conducive to creativity. The workshop began with some sensory games, which were designed to generate powerful and descriptive images that could eventually lead to poems. Much of the workshop time was spent individually, with students gauging their

Continued on next page

own progress, working with one another and a staff member from time to time. The workshop culminated with the compilation of a book. Students entered all of the work on computers, designed a cover for their book, and distributed it to the Institute community.

MUSIC

This workshop introduced students to the concepts of musical improvisation and composition. The group worked with Orff percussion instruments, xylophones, and recorders to learn the basic skills and concepts involved in working in a music ensemble, including meter, rhythm, major and minor scales, and intervals. Several days were spent working on pieces composed for a small percussion group; later, participants composed their own pieces that they shared with the others. The group worked on accompaniments for several Institute songs, playing along while the rest of the students sang after meals.

PHOTOGRAPHY

This workshop began with an introduction to the 35-millimeter camera. Students experimented with the different lens functions and then paired off to begin taking photographs. The emphasis was on portraits and composition. Many photographers visited other workshops to take pictures of students in action. The next step was to learn each stage of developing black-and-white film. Students

mixed and set up the chemicals, processed the film, and printed from the negatives. Acquiring these skills was not easy, and most students initially found their film over- or underexposed. Once everyone had successfully developed negatives, the group focused on print quality and experimenting with composition and contrast. The photography workshop became an important part of the newspaper workshop.

DRAMA

The drama workshop brought together a diverse group of participants with and without dramatic experience. Students in this workshop shared a desire to create and perform in a theatrical production. The first few sessions were spent doing warm-up theater exercises and improvisation games to increase everyone's comfort level. Soon the group became cohesive and expressive as they worked on ideas for plays. They decided to do a play pertaining to education, concentrating on the students' own experiences in junior high and high school. The play was performed for the entire group during an evening program.

FLIGHT

The flight workshop brought together several themes, including heavier-than-air devices, woodworking, model-building, and flight itself. The group began their model-building by experimenting with objects of different weights and designs; then they made different types of planes by paperfolding. Based on what they learned about the paper airplanes, individual participants then each designed and decorated a balsa-wood model aircraft. Students presented their designs and finished models to the Institute community, explaining the planning and process involved in building them.

JOURNALISM

Students in the journalism workshop were in charge of creating and publishing the Institute newspaper, the *Panopticon*. Various tasks were distributed among the members during the first workshop session. Participants could choose to work on news reporting, editorials, creative writing, personal ads, page layout, typing, editing, or cover design. During the final session, this group collaborated with students in the photography workshop and the creative-writing group to produce the final draft of the newspaper. The *Panopticon* was distributed to every Institute participant and staff member.

ANTHROPOLOGY

This workshop focused on learning the history and skills of several native cultures. By learning some of the living skills of Eskimos and various other Native-American tribes, for example,

students increased their awareness and appreciation of different cultures. First, they explored fire making, learning how to start fires without matches by using two different techniques. Next the group learned how to make rope from plant and tree fibers and practiced primitive animal-stalking techniques. The students used branches, twine, rocks, and a tarp to construct an Indian sweat lodge (a type of primitive sauna) at the Institute site. They also took a field trip to a nearby natural history museum.

STAINED GLASS

Each student in this workshop began by using simple geometric shapes to make a two-dimensional design of a window. Next, students learned how to use such tools as the glass cutter, router, and pliers to cut various shapes of colored glass to fit their design patterns. They then joined the glass, using copper tape and lead channel. Concepts from geometry, physics, and chemistry surfaced throughout this workshop. Projects were framed and finished with hanging wire, and each participant presented his or her window to the rest of the Institute community.

eration. Work projects benefit the Institute community as a whole— by physically enhancing the facility (as when students built a bridge and added a balcony to the barn) or by providing new resources (as when students created a running trail and constructed an additional potter's wheel). When students and staff join together in designing an organic garden, fixing a hay wagon, or creating a lighting system, they are directly engaged in a number of processes that are essential in many real-life situations:

- Planning

- Learning new skills

- Organizing a large task

- Testing new concepts

- Solving problems

- Learning from mistakes

- Making friends by working together

- Sharing finished products

New work projects are started every session. Although most are completed in the course of the month-long Institute, some of the larger projects take more than one Institute session to finish. Some projects are complex, requiring mathematical computations and the acquisition of technical or practical skills. Others are simpler, requiring only the repetition of one or two basic skills.

In work projects, when they learn that they can plan and physically accomplish something that has a visible impact on their community, students develop positive attitudes toward work.

Whether simple or complex, long- or short-term, completed projects are generally a great source of pride and satisfaction for everyone involved. Students learn that they can plan and physically accomplish something that has a visible impact on their community. They develop positive attitudes toward work, seeing work for what it is—an opportunity for problem solving, collaboration, and sustained physical effort that can yield satisfying results.

Staff, like participants, come to High/Scope with various levels of work experience. Some have never built anything but find that they can call on experiences with gardening, decoration, sewing, design, or camping. Others come with previous construction or engineering experience and feel very comfortable guiding young people through the many steps of building something such as a bridge or a lifeguard chair. Each staff member receives the support and assistance necessary to lead a work project successfully. Often two staff members are paired to take advantage of their complementary skills (a person skilled in construction might be paired with an artist, for example).

At the beginning of each work project session, staff and students plan together to

- Determine the basic outcome sought in the work project

- Decide on the "givens" of the project (location, size, funds available, materials required)

- Generate a design/blueprint/diagram/model

- Break the work into subparts, so small groups can work on different tasks simultaneously

- Sequence the subparts and organize the materials and tools

Planning takes time but provides students and staff with a clear vision of their goals. Planning allows them to proceed from one step to the next without waiting for someone to tell them what to do. Participants who are less skilled than others can see how their contribution fits into the overall project. Students who want to take on leadership have a concrete basis for doing so.

With the help of careful planning and structuring on the part of staff, students can see their ideas and designs materialize. They become interested in how the world around them is put together and aware of the efforts that have gone into making the buildings, roads, furniture, tools, and other objects of the material world. For an idea of what students accomplish in work projects, see "Examples of Past Work Projects" on the next page.

EXAMPLES OF PAST WORK PROJECTS

- **Canoe Pond Dock.** The dock of the canoe pond was taken out of the water, and a new foundation was poured. The dock was reinforced and replaced, so its level would fluctuate with the level of the pond.

- **Stucco Causeway.** This was a landscaping project in which the students repaired the rock wall between the two boys' houses and landscaped the embarkment leading down into the valley.

- **Art Deck Stairs.** The group designed and fabricated a short stairway that led from the art room drawing-deck to the lawn.

- **Dining Room Steps/Landscaping.** This group first replaced the dislodged boulders of the first step at the entrance to the dining hall. They then went on to tackle a variety of landscaping tasks throughout the facility.

- **Ballet Bar/Display Case.** A small group repaired the ballet bar and modified, attached, and wired a dozen lighted display cases that will be used to display students' products.

- **Garden.** A small group of students tended the garden—planting, weeding, and marking the rows of vegetables.

- **Recycling.** This group organized and implemented a comprehensive recycling program for the entire facility. They installed storage systems and produced a user's guide for future groups.

Evening Programs

Most students would not describe evening programs as instructional times. They see them instead as "fun " activities for the Institute community. But evening programs *are* part of the overall educational strategy of the Institute—exposing students to new ideas, providing successful large-group and whole-community experiences, creating a shared culture, teaching new skills, and providing opportunities to explore new realms.

Evening programs, which are planned by staff members in their weekly meetings, fall into several categories, including the following:

- *Musicale*—This is a once-a-week evening of small-group

(or individual) musical or dramatic performances. The performances often stem from clubs, workshops, self-scheduled times, or room group activities.

- *Council*—Modeled after the Quaker meeting, this is a once-a-week evening of quiet reflection and sharing around a campfire. A council meeting starts with everyone gathering to walk silently through the fields to a clearing up on a hill. Then there is a short presentation or reading to stimulate thought about a certain topic, such as peer pressure. Individual students are free to share their thoughts and insights, allowing silence to fall for a few minutes after each person speaks.

- *Folk dance*—Folk dance plays a special community-building role at the Institute. At least one evening a week is dedicated to learning and practicing new dances.

- *Problem-solving games*—Students engage in various activities, such as the "shopping" game described in Chapter 1.

- *Skits or improvisations*—These include such things as miming scientific processes or acting out fairy tales.

- *Special nights*—These are times for presentations of special topics (such as college night, international night) and for student-led programs.

Field Trips

Students typically go on two field trips during the month-long Institute session. These outings are designed around specific program objectives.

The first objective is to develop career awareness among students. A key part of this is exposure to postsecondary education opportunities. A field trip to a nearby university provides students with active exposure to a college setting. In the past, the group has visited the University of Michigan, touring various schools, classrooms, lecture halls, libraries, bookstores, and residence halls. The participants split into small groups that are led by staff members; since staff members are themselves former or current college students, they are able to share personal experiences and insights about higher education.

Another objective is to expose students to cultural elements that are not typically part of popular teen culture. While staff address this objective in a general way throughout the month, they also try to include a field trip to an art museum or a live theater production. Such real-world experiences help to reinforce the idea that students can carry over their interests at the Institute to participate in similar activities back home.

Discussion and other preparatory activities before the field trips help students to think through their expectations. Follow-up activities help students to sort out their impressions, to integrate what they have seen and learned, and to articulate some goals for themselves.

Special Workshops

We have found that some areas of exploration—careers, folk dance, and health—are of value to all students. Therefore staff offer workshops in these areas to the whole group during a special workshop week. Typically, two of these special workshops take place simultaneously, with each half of the community attending one for the first part of the morning and then switching to attend the other for the second part of the morning. Alternatively, staff may set aside a two- or three-day period for the whole community to focus on a special topic, with a variety of related activities and small-group offerings to allow students to explore, to encounter new ideas and possibilities, and to share insights with one another.

The college and career workshop. Toward the end of each Institute session the whole community participates in a three-day workshop that deals specifically with career development, problem solving, college and career awareness, and further exploration of postsecondary options. Offered in a spirit of fun, creativity, and exploration, this workshop includes many different activities that enable students to contemplate, prioritize, and plan for their own futures. Students sometimes engage in an extensive role-play exercise in which each student creates and acts out a unique personality that includes job, income, life-style, budget, and family characteristics. A student interacts as that person in a variety of contexts. The focus of the exercise is on setting goals and thinking through the kinds of responsibilities that arise for that fictional person over several years.

The folk dance workshop. One of the highlights of the High/Scope Institute is the accelerated training each student receives in international folk dancing. During a very short period of time, students learn numerous basic and intermediate-level folk dances.

Learning together about international folk dancing, an activity most students have not experienced before coming to the Institute, provides students with a common ground. It is taught in a way that enables every individual to experience success and enjoyment. Some participants arrive at the Institute unable even to recognize or move to a simple beat. But by the end of the folk dance workshop, nearly all are capable of coordinating their movements to music and performing a variety of dances from around the world.

Needless to say, students end up feeling extremely pleased and impressed with themselves—both individually and collectively. We have also observed a curious phenomenon over the years: The folk dance workshop has consistently served as a critical turning point in both group and individual development; the workshop seems to lead students to a sense of cooperation and community—to the belief that together they can accomplish great things.

The health workshop. The health workshop consists of five sessions, attended by all students, in which health issues are actively explored. The staff members responsible for planning the workshop try to find activities that raise awareness of key health topics, such as first aid, sexually transmitted diseases, alcohol and drug abuse, environmental hazards, and preventative health practices. By encouraging students to share what they know, to formulate questions, and to raise one another's awareness, the workshop helps them to see health as a dynamic, personally relevant topic. They come to see that good health entails knowledge, attitudes, choices, and practices. The workshop often helps students to realize that they have the ability to gather necessary information, to use health resources (including written materials and health care professionals), to get appropriate information, and to understand their personal health needs.

Activities often include participating in health-related simulation games; creating skits to explore reactions to health-related challenges; writing and designing public health messages for radio announcements, video clips, newspaper articles, and other media; and engaging in panel discussions, debates, and group investigations.

• • •

Each program activity described here adds a unique dimension to the overall Institute experience, contributing to the active learning and interdisciplinary style of the instruction. Figure 3.2 on pp. 90–91 provides an example of a typical month-long calendar of activities.

Materials and Resources

The High/Scope Institute for IDEAS aims to provide teenagers with a rich environment. This is not necessarily synonymous with a costly environment, though anyone who has directed a program knows that access to funds for plentiful supplies is certainly helpful. A rich environment, however, is created by providing four kinds of resources:

- **Physical spaces** that allow for group work, physical activity, safety, mess-making, and multiple activities

- **Plentiful materials and tools** that promote exploration, active use, and creative endeavors

- **Staff members** who are multifaceted, able to apply their academic knowledge to real-world tasks, and able to share their knowledge and interests in a mentoring way

- **An atmosphere,** created through the program structure and the attitudes of the staff and participants, **that values both individuals and community**—an atmosphere of trust, exploration, acceptance of mistakes, recognition of many forms of success and many styles of contribution

Of these four items, the last two are the most important. It is possible to make do with raw materials scavenged from around town and hand-me-down equipment that is not necessarily the latest technology. It is also possible to get by with less than ideal space, if people are creative and cooperative about using it. But without the guidance of supportive adults and without an atmosphere of affirmation and investigation, a learning environment is likely to be inadequate for stimulating adolescents' active learning.

A visit to the facility of the High/Scope Institute is a bit like an archeological expedition: All around, one sees evidence of the "earlier cultures" of the program. At the entrance is a cross section of a log that was inscribed with the High/Scope insignia by one of the program's first groups of students, back in the early 1960s. Alongside it is a retaining wall and a garden designed and planted by another group of students in the late 1980s. Everywhere there is evidence of the efforts of past participants: a suspension bridge; a totem pole designed and carved by students in the first few summers of the program; a covered bridge converted from an old corn crib; a two-story balcony on the back of the barn; a triangular gazebo structure hanging high in the trees, with a suspended walkway leading up to it; and on an isthmus stretching into the pond, a sundial clearly marking the march of time. There are also numerous benches, meeting areas, and an outdoor stage platform overlooking the canoeing pond. These projects have provided successive groups of Institute students with a great sense of pride and competence while at the same time passing on lasting resources to future students.

The materials and supplies used at the Institute reflect the program's active learning philosophy. The facility is made up of well-stocked program areas. These include an art area, a science and nature area, a shop and electronics room, a computer area, a photography darkroom, an office area, a costume room, and a polished dance floor and theatrical performance space in the old barn (with adjacent nooks and crannies).

There are also many indoor and outdoor general-use areas, such as the side lawn, the "island," two small ponds, recreation rooms, a fire ring, picnic tables, sports fields, a tipi (student-built in 1993), hayfields, and garden areas.

FIGURE 3.2

HIGH/SCOPE INSTITUTE FOR IDEAS CALENDAR: MAY 1993 SESSION

SUNDAY	MONDAY	TUESDAY	WEDNESDAY
9 Staff arrive	**10**	**11**	**12**
16 Club A Club A Personal Crests	**17** Club B Club B Folk dancing	**18** Club B Work project Paper Towers	**19** Club B Work project Musicale
23 Informal morning Student-led clubs Storytelling	**24** University of Michigan trip Council	**25** Workshop A Workshop A Folk dancing	**26** Work project Workshop A Self-propelled Vehicles
30 Informal/cleaning Visitors College Night	**31** Folk dance/Careers Service Musicale	**1** Folk dance/Careers Workshop B Las Fallas	**2** Folk dance/Health Work project Measurement/estimation
6 Informal morning Student-led clubs Community Service*	**7** Workshop B Workshop B Scavenger Hunt	**8** Workshop B Workshop B Space Dancing*	**9** Workshop B Workshop B Musicale

* Indicates ⅓ of Institute group are on day-long canoe trip.

THURSDAY	**FRIDAY**	**SATURDAY**
13	**14**	**15** Students arrive Rotation activity Eco-mapping
20 Work project Workshop A Communications games	**21** Work project Workshop A Science skits	**22** Workship A Workshop A Egg Drop
27 Community meeting Student-led clubs Shopping Game	**28** Disease Transmission Simulation Student-led clubs Council	**29** Workshop A Workshop A Fractured Fairytales
3 Folk dance/Health Workshop B Council	**4** Folk dance/Health Work project Group Roles	**5** Workshop B Workshop B Folk dancing*
10 Cleaning Musicale Ghost Stone council	**11** Students leave Staff evaluations	**12** Staff leave

Materials and supplies invite students to be active; they stimulate exploration and hands-on creativity. When coupled with staff support to integrate planning, problem solving, reflection, and evaluation, they provide students with a rich basis for developing knowledge, competency, self-confidence, and ongoing curiosity about the world and how it works.

It is sometimes a challenge for the Institute director to find human resources. In a world where higher education often emphasizes a theoretical approach, it is not always easy to find college students and recent graduates who know how to apply their knowledge in active and interactive ways. Also, it is not always easy (but well worth the effort) to find staff who come from diverse backgrounds (similar to those of Institute students) and who have become successful, well-rounded people.

The High/Scope Institute is a challenge and a learning experience for its staff as well as its students. Staff members are asked to use their knowledge and expertise in creating applied, interdisciplinary activities. For some, who may be quite educated in their respective fields, this is difficult. It calls for imagination, enthusiasm, energy, flexibility, and willingness to learn.

Despite all obstacles, High/Scope has managed year after year to find wonderful young adults who are challenged by the opportunity to share their knowledge and enthusiasm with teenagers. Each staff has its unique set of competencies and strengths, and so each Institute session has a character all its own. But High/Scope does strive in its staff recruitment to consistently cover certain bases. Each year, there are eight program areas in which the director attempts to ensure staff expertise or experience: music, art, drama, dance, science and computers, nature, construction/engineering, and media (photography, video, etc.).

A staff member with expertise in a given area needs to have a well-rounded familiarity with the processes, tools, and concepts most used, as well as enthusiasm for learning more about the area. The staff person with musical expertise, for example, needs to be able to teach a wide repertoire of folk and international songs, to be able to work at a basic level in a variety of musical modes, and to have a multicultural awareness of the uses and potential of music. She or he does not need to be a highly skilled performer or a brilliant theorist but should be able to teach music as an active, living medium to students at a basic level.

Because it is ideal to have a well-rounded set of offerings for clubs and workshops, the director also looks for staff with multiple interests and talents, people who would like to branch out, to experiment, and to offer a variety of types of instruction. Each staff member is called on to be a competent generalist—to be able to lead a work project or facilitate an evening program that may have nothing to do with any one particular area of expertise.

"What Kinds of People Staff the Institute?" on the next page describes the abilities and interests of some typical staff members.

Psychological and Physical Safety

In order to thrive and develop constructive attitudes and behaviors, teenagers need to be psychologically and physically safe. Unfortunately, many young people (and adults) are forced to function within settings that do not protect them and do not support their physical and psychological well-being.

Safety is more than the absence of physical threat and the absence of active abuse, although many teenagers are relieved to experience even this measure of it. Safety implies that there are consistent and reasonable supports, responsible interactions, well-defined and well-implemented mechanisms for allowing all members of a community to participate positively.

Consider some of the following conditions. Teenagers (or young children, or adults) are unsafe

- If they fear physical violence

- If they fear emotional insult, blackmail, or denigration

- If they live in unsanitary conditions, fail to eat nutritious foods, are at the mercy of others' imbalance or illness (including alcoholic behaviors and erratic tempers)

- If they are pressured to engage in behaviors that are frightening or uncomfortable

WHAT KINDS OF PEOPLE STAFF THE INSTITUTE?

John is a folk musician and high school English teacher from San Francisco. In addition to music, teaching, and San Francisco, his interests include art, science, camping, traveling, animals and building things out of wood. He has worked at the Institute since 1989.

Katrina is a struggling artist and musician living in New York City. She can often be seen making her way through the Manhattan subway turnstiles with her cello and portfolio. She began working at High/Scope while pursuing degrees in literature and fine arts at Michigan State University. She enjoys working with students on pottery, monoprinting, painting, and papermaking.

Will finished his secondary teaching certificate last year, but instead of teaching, he currently works as a naturalist and volunteers in a state-run counseling center for youth. He loves being outdoors, playing his guitar, and listening to young people.

Shelly is pursuing a Ph.D. in urban planning while helping High/Scope start a replication of the Institute in Ohio. Formerly city manager of a small Ohio town, Shelly's interests include community development, politics, art, and her dog.

Tanisha comes from nearby Detroit. Her main interests are music and dance, and she is currently finishing a fine arts degree in dance from the University of Michigan. When not in class or at the Institute, she works in a group home for teenaged mothers.

Diego is a biologist from Bogotá, Colombia. While in Michigan pursuing a master's degree in natural resources, he has worked at two sessions of the Institute. Also a photographer, he splits his time at the Institute between the photo and science labs.

Elizabeth came to the Institute from California, where she was working on integrating students with disabilities into mainstream educational settings. At the Institute, she can often be found working in the art room or leading theatrical explorations in the barn.

Andy began as a High/Scope "camper" in 1985. He has since returned as a staff member for five Institute sessions. Skilled in woodworking and several art media, Andy can usually be found making something. When not making things, he's usually reading, as he is on his way to a Ph.D. in Latin American literature.

- If they are marginalized or made to feel that their contributions are of no value

- If they are unable to express themselves constructively

- If they do not have positive role models and loving, healthy attention from adults

- If they are caught up in addictive or rote behaviors, including the use of drugs, alcohol, or cigarettes and excessive use of radio or TV

In presenting these unsafe conditions, we wish to emphasize that safety depends not only on having emotional and physical supports but also on being able to express oneself, to find affirmation and membership, and to take care of oneself within a given context.

The High/Scope Institute is fortunate to be geographically located in a safe, rural setting where the crime rate is low and the physical resources are clean and well-maintained. The adequate financial support for the Institute ensures that each member of the Institute community is well housed, well fed, and well cared for.

This does not describe the situation for many of the Institute's teenagers when they are back home. The disadvantages they suffer in their home communities often leave them shut down, defensive, nervous, wary, anxious, or overly aggressive. Staff face a special challenge in trying to provide supportive, consistent adult responses while helping teenagers to become safe to themselves and one another.

High/Scope's institutional response to the issue of safety is woven into every aspect of the program:

- *Consistency* is provided through a well-defined schedule and clearly articulated practices.

- *Clear guidelines* are provided for healthy and supportive adult interaction with young people; staff are trained to help teenagers experience a good balance of autonomy and guidance.

- *Choices* are continually offered, enabling teenagers to pursue and express interests.

- *Clear policies and expectations* exclude the use of drugs, alcohol, or tobacco and other addictive activities for both participants and staff.

- *A sense of community* is promoted at all times, with active integration of races, ages, and genders in contexts where the differences can be appreciated, recognized, and celebrated.

- *Success is redefined,* allowing each individual to experience success in his or her own way.

- *Cooperation* and collaboration are promoted as goals within all activities, making sure that everyone can find a way to contribute.

- *Multiple opportunities for communication* are provided within each day and within each activity; teenagers have opportunities to test their perceptions and expand their understanding of the reasons for and dimensions of the experiences offered at the Institute.

- *Regular affirmation and support* of individuals teaches students to appreciate one another's unique contributions.

- *Exploration of values* encourages students to articulate what they need for themselves and from others in order to feel heard, understood, and appreciated. Certain safety-promoting values are stressed—open-mindedness, tolerance of differences, and inclusiveness.

- *Tools for achievement* are offered to each individual: planning, action, problem solving, reflection, and artistic expression that allows for fuller experience.

The High/Scope Institute does not offer its young people psychotherapy in response to their troubles; it is not designed to do that. But ironically, the program often has a profound therapeutic effect on teenagers who have experienced dysfunction in their home environments. The reason is that the elements provided by the Institute are similar to the elements of good parenting: consistency, loving attention, guidance, clear rules and expectations with steady enforcement, and support for autonomy.

By engaging in regular, wholesome activities in a setting designed to be healthy and socially and emotionally nurturing, students have a chance to achieve an equilibrium within themselves, and between themselves and others. In this context, most are successful, and many make exponential leaps in their understanding and ability to live constructively.

Expectations for Individuals, Groups, and the Program as a Whole

The quality of any experience is greatly affected by the expectations participants bring to it. Thus great care is taken at the Institute to convey expectations to both staff and students and to give them opportunities to recognize and clarify their own expectations.

Two types of expectations are especially helpful at the Institute: One type includes the "rules" that spell out the behaviors and attitudes excluded from this particular community. For example, shaming or making fun of peers is not accepted. The second type of expectation includes attitudinal stances to be taken—for example, that success is something all students should be helped to experience during their month at the Institute.

Rules and Policies

As already mentioned, High/Scope believes that alcohol, drugs, tobacco, radio, TV, and junk foods are too dangerous, distracting, or disruptive to belong in a setting where students are being asked to try new behaviors and learn new patterns of interacting. The directors explain this requirement when recruiting Institute participants. They ask each student to sign a "contract" signaling an agreement to leave these things behind for the month. Staff, too, are asked to abstain from these distractions.

Ironically, while this requirement is seen as difficult by some, it tends to make many teenagers curious and interested in what they will experience. As one participant put it, "When I heard I had to come without my cigarettes and music, I thought, 'How will I make it?' My friends teased me and said I'd never make it. But I told them I was sure I could."

Since the Institute is only a month-long program, in a setting that is radically different from what most of the students are used to back home, it is a wonderful opportunity for experimentation; in the absence of bombardment by popular culture or adult culture, young people can create a culture of their own.

Most of the limits that are set at the Institute involve concerns about safety or about including each individual in the formation of community. While some students gripe about the limits, they also defend those limits when called on to deliberate about them. For example, one summer in the early 1970s two students showed up with marijuana and were sneaking off to smoke it, encouraging certain others to join them. This behavior quickly came to the attention of staff, who realized that students who did not wish to join this clique were upset about the behavior but also afraid to report it to staff.

Staff members called a whole-community meeting to discuss the problem, without singling out the two individuals by name. After much discussion about how divisive the practice was and how angry some students felt who were sticking to the rules, the community decided by consensus to ask the drug users to flush their supplies down the toilet or agree to leave the Institute. This solution worked, and the two students admitted later that they had been relieved to be given support from the community, instead of just receiving punishment from the directors. They confessed that they hadn't realized their behavior might be upsetting to others or that it might affect the whole community. When they could see that it did, they were willing to comply with the policy.

Teenagers like to test limits and at the same time make decisions for themselves. Staff members present expectations in a way that makes logical sense to students, and when individuals push the limits or break the rules, they are helped to see the impact on the community or on their own safety. Many of the participants are stunned by this approach, because they are used to being punished (physically or verbally) or rejected by adults.

Students are taken aback, and then pleased, when staff respond to misbehavior with equanimity. When Jemiel was distracting others during the planning of a work project in the garden, for example, the staff member, instead of punishing him, suggested that he record the planning process with the video camera. This helped him to refocus his energy and find a way to engage in the project on a different level. It also kept Jemiel integrated with the group, which evidently is not what usually happens to him in his school setting. Jemiel claimed that at school, he spends more time in the vice principal's office than in classes.

As another example of how staff implement Institute policies, the Institute director reported a heartwarming incident from a recent session:

● ● ●

Brad was a participant who came from a dysfunctional home. He had even experienced some broken bones as a result of physical abuse by his step-father. When Brad first arrived at the Institute, there were several incidents in which he threatened to hit other students. His room counselor spent time talking with him about why violence (and threatening violence) was not an acceptable response to his frustration.

On Saturday night, when staff members were having their first weekly meeting and students were asked to monitor their own behaviors (with occasional visits from staff), Brad showed up at the meeting in his pajamas. The other members of his room group trailed in behind him. With great trepidation, the director went over to find out what was wrong.

Brad said: "We were having a disagreement, and I really want to hit John. But I know I'm not supposed to use violence, and I can't think of what else to do."

Brad's room counselor spent a few minutes brainstorming with the group about what Brad could do, instead of slugging his roommate John. They wrote a list and took it back to their room for Brad (and the others) to use as a resource the next time they got angry with one another. For Brad, this amount of self-control and self-awareness was quite a breakthrough. It was perhaps the first time he had asked adults or peers for help in handling a situation he didn't have the skill to handle.

● ● ●

Couples and Exclusive Relationships

One of the most challenging and challenged Institute policies is the stance on exclusive relationships. Many programs either turn a blind eye to the formation of romantic couples or else forbid it outright and punish offenders. At High/Scope we feel that as in everything else, the complications of coeducation offer students an opportunity to rethink their attitudes and to learn new ways of interacting.

To be a teenager in American society today is a difficult task. Pressure to become sexually active and romantically involved starts very early and can be very strong. The media send teens mixed messages, showering them with warnings against certain behaviors and then seemingly at the same time promoting those behaviors. Adult role models in many of the students' lives send similar mixed messages.

While some attitudes have changed during the last three decades, images of stereotypical female and male behavior are still pervasive. Teenagers come to the Institute with a very wide range of social, economic, and cultural attitudes and experiences. The Institute personnel must walk a fine line between respecting cultural attitudes and promoting belief in the equality of opportunities for girls and boys.

One of the most important aspects of the Institute is the freedom it gives individuals to make choices. And yet, because of the program's public commitment, it also must operate in a way that conforms with the expectations of conservative parents and organizations and that ensures young people's safety. One of the ways the Institute addresses this need is in the form of supervision. The daily schedule of activities is a full one, and participants are expected to choose from among the activities provided or to design their own activities; they do *not* have the option of nonparticipation—of hanging out on their own or segregating themselves from the community in couples. This policy is articulated early on in the program and reinforced by ongoing staff support for each student to find ways to be part of the daily routine of activities.

Perhaps the main challenge continuously faced by staff members is deciding when and how to respond to (or interfere with) the development of "young love," which is after all a normal developmental task for this age group. Shouldn't boys and girls of this age have the opportunity to experience, in the safe setting of Institute life, whatever kinds of emotional attachment or infatuation are possible? It is not unheard of for young people who have met at this age to grow up, marry, and become productive citizens in their communities.

A number of events in the past have influenced High/Scope's view of couples at the Institute. One major event occurred early in the development of the program, when the policy toward couples was more liberal than it is today:

• • •

A school bus was used to transport Institute students to attend a play at a nearby university. As students gathered on the bus, they sat wherever they chose. It turned out that "couples" sat together, and others not "going with anyone" sat elsewhere. After attending the play, the couples led a charge back to the bus and lined up at the door, wanting to grab the seats at the back, for greater privacy.

It became clear that the whole Institute group had organized themselves into a social hierarchy. The most popular students, who had formed couple relationships, were first by the bus door. They were followed by some younger students who had followed the lead of the older students and formed couples that seemed to be based more on appearance than affection. Last in line were the remaining students—those who had not yet developed a social sense, those who were "misfits," those who were being left out in this couple climate.

• • •

The lesson from this experience was clear: If permitted, a social hierarchy of this type could easily form. In such a climate, staff members would be wasting effort trying to engage students in educational and broadening activities—the majority would already be otherwise engaged.

To change this, a clearer policy about couples was developed. Staff members let young people know that there was no policy discouraging two students from forming a special friendship, be it a close friendship of two girls, two boys, or a boy and a girl. What they discussed with students, however, was how to *handle* such friendships.

The requirements of the Institute are that couples or "best friends" must remain active in the program; they must interact with others regularly, as well as with their special friends. This means that all students go to workshops and projects, participate in work teams, and remain actively involved in the activities and productions of the program. In the natural course of random or staff-designed groupings, this also means there are many group experiences in which a given couple is not together.

Teenagers at the Institute often find it difficult to understand this request for active involvement. In their high schools and in the patterns understood at home, a couple is a dating arrangement that is often sanctioned and frequently used as a defense against the world—against parents, teachers, high school rules and regulations. Being in a couple often enables a young person to avoid having to maintain relationships with a range of people. Thus the couple is a special kind of institution with well-defined rules. The Institute guidelines disrupt this pattern, confusing some of the young people who interpret our policy as High/Scope "forbidding romance."

One important reason why the formation of exclusive couples is discouraged lies in the Institute's goal of getting young people to experience new challenges. Exclusive relationships are discouraged for much the same reason that watching TV or listening to the radio are discouraged: These are behaviors that the teenagers are likely to experience extensively while *not* at the Institute. Thus, while they have the unique opportunities that the Institute provides to engage in new activities, learn new skills, and interact with both teens and adults in what is often a new way, students should be unencumbered so they can take full advantage of these.

This policy tends to disrupt a pattern often seen with teenagers: the submerging of one person's abilities and interests in those of the other. It is very disappointing, for example, to watch a talented young woman do well the first week or so of the Institute and then fall into a couple situation in which she becomes more concerned with watching her boyfriend participate in an activity than with participating herself. The reverse can also occur. A young man may get distracted by an infatuation and, instead of thinking for himself, follow the lead of his girlfriend in choosing program offerings. Couple relationships, if not guided into healthy patterns, can change the participants' focus dramatically. Students often lose interest in activities and in getting to know others; they more easily give up personal initiative; and they tend to focus on how to "escape" together into their own private world.

Of course, another worry that parents have in sending their children to a residential program is that someone might get pregnant (or be exposed to a sexually transmitted disease) owing to a failure of adult supervision or guidance. Physical interaction of a sexual nature is not permitted at the Institute, and staff members supervise to insure that it does not occur. This rule applies equally to staff and participants.

The main issue of sex and sex differences addressed at the Institute has to do with the roles and role training individual boys and girls gain within the context. The basic goal of the program is to provide equality for all individuals to try any activity and undertake any type of program that they wish without regard to existing stereotypes. Policies about couples and social relationships at the Institute are driven principally by that goal.

Setting Positive Expectations for Students

Punishment does not exist at the Institute—at least in any form recognizable to the participants. Students who are acting out are helped to refocus their efforts on something constructive. Students who are breaking rules are asked to stop and are helped to think about their actions and the impact of those actions on others—sometimes in the context of a small group, a room group, or even the whole community, and sometimes in private discussion with a staff member or director. Only occasionally do staff members encounter a student who is so focused on antisocial or destructive behavior, and so unable to change it, that he or she is asked to choose between changing that behavior and going home.

The positive atmosphere created by the Institute's high expectations for students acts as a strong disincentive to misbehavior. This atmosphere of high expectations is based on our beliefs, listed here:

- Individuals can make a unique and valuable contribution to this community, and all efforts are focused on helping students discover what their potential is.

- Teenagers are capable of great things: understanding complicated processes, creating delightful art pieces, working together to solve problems in mature and sensitive ways.

- Each member of the community, among both students and staff, has a contributing role. It is not acceptable in this setting for one person's domination (be that person a staff member or student) to block another's participation.

- Students learn best by experiencing trial and error, by exploring, by turning problems or obstacles into challenges. All staff interactions with young people reflect this attitude.

- Young people are at the Institute to enjoy themselves and to be supported in their individual development. There is no hidden checklist of academic concepts or achievements that will be used to grade or judge the students' performance.

- Students need authentic choices and activities that excite them, that capture their imaginations, and that stimulate them to explore new realms. Staff incorporate this attitude into their ongoing planning sessions.

- A program needs to be designed in response to the particular students who attend. While some popular activities are offered year after year, the primary goal is to create a program that supports each particular group of individuals and their specific evolution. Thus students feel that the program belongs to them. They tend to participate enthusiastically in the offerings and develop willingness to try new things.

- While students are encouraged to be sensitive to other's feelings and respectful of their beliefs, the focus is on action and community building as a response to difficulties that arise. Thus, when two students have an argument, they are encouraged to reach a mutual understanding and resolve their difficulties, rather than to focus solely on what they feel and why they feel that way.

- Staff members work hard to influence the peer pressure at the Institute to take positive forms. Thus students might form a small group to support someone in trying something difficult.

- The successful, engaged communities of past Institute sessions have a subtle, positive influence on present participants. Students quickly pick up that this is a great experience, a wonderful opportunity, and a "cool" place to be. That expectation carries them through doubtful moments, when they are struggling with uncomfortable interactions or difficult personal growth.

Adult Participation—Expectations for Staff

Unlike many residential programs, staff members are "on duty" most of the time. (They do, of course, get a few days and evenings off during each Institute session.) Each staff member is an instructor, room counselor, table counselor, role model, mentor, participant, learner, and resource person—continuously from morning until night. While this is a demanding and often exhausting responsibility, it is a necessary one. Adults are authentic, full-time, fully participating members of the Institute community, not distant authority-figures or teachers.

Staff members, as part of the community being formed by students and staff alike, must function as a productive group. The Institute program, no matter how well developed over the years, is not a formula that works on its own. Staff members *make* each session of the Institute successful by planning appropriate activities, by creating and sustaining the historic Institute culture, and by interacting in positive ways with the students and with one another.

Directors remind staff that it is necessary to provide students not only with *individual* role models but also with a *group* role model by acting together in cohesive, cooperative, and effective ways. The staff is supported in developing this group image through a week of intensive training, which is structured like a mini-Institute, with expectations and scheduling similar to those of the students' program.

Staff members are generally mature enough to handle the expectations just described. Their relative youth, however, is also an advantage. Unlike many adults who have worked for years on their own as classroom teachers, the young-adult staff members are generally able to readily embrace the team concept.

Because staff are responsible for creating and maintaining the Institute culture, they must be constantly aware of what kinds of behavior and activity they are modeling for students. If staff members swear, students will be inclined to swear. If staff members sneak off to listen to the radio or smoke cigarettes, students will see them as hypocrites. The same is true of talking when someone else is trying to talk, or deciding not to sing when the whole group is singing. All of the expectations set up for students must be met consistently by staff.

Intensive training prior to the Institute as well as ongoing support from directors helps staff to plan appropriate activities and to set and maintain high expectations for student behavior.

Because forming exclusive relationships, rifts, power struggles, and competition are discouraged among the participating students, staff are also asked to work with these same principles, so they can function most effectively.

When issues do come up, such as interpersonal problems or concerns about a staff member's behavior or style of interaction, such problems are addressed immediately. If problems or concerns are not dealt with in a timely and productive manner, they not only affect the individual staff member's experience but also ripple quickly outward to the students and the program as a whole.

Staff training does not end on the Saturday morning after training week, when the students arrive. A great deal of information is passed along during the pre-Institute training, and countless situations are thought through and planned by the staff ahead of time. However, once the program begins, there are always more activities to be planned, issues and individual students to be discussed, problems to be solved, and responsibilities to be distributed.

Throughout the Institute month, the staff meets every morning before breakfast, to touch base with one another, to verify plans for the day and evening programs, to discuss any visitors or special situations that may be scheduled, and to relate successes and share individual concerns. Some meetings last longer than others. On one day a specific training topic or issue might be discussed at length; on another day a meeting might last only 15 minutes.

Staff members also meet at length on Saturday nights following lights out. At the Saturday meeting, considered the major meeting of the week, staff members address the needs of individual participants, discussing in depth any issues that have arisen. The staff reflects on the events of the past week and plans for the upcoming week.

It would be misleading, however, to represent Saturday night staff meetings as entirely serious business. These meetings tend to be enjoyable times for staff to assemble, to have some fun together, to share one another's successes and failures, and to renew their collective energy and enthusiasm for the upcoming week.

Throughout the Institute program, staff members assume the following roles:

- **Facilitators**—responsible for structuring the learning environment and organizing the appropriate materials, tools, and concepts

- **Listeners**—willing to listen to students attentively and responsively; able to recognize the intent behind students' words and the impact of students' comments on one another

- **Observers**—able to observe students' actions, behaviors, and nonverbal communications and to reflect this back to them in constructive ways; able to see what students understand, perceive, and need, and to respond appropriately

- **Encouragers**—able to help students, in ways that are not overbearing, to take risks and venture out from their comfortable domains; able to help students proceed forward during times of temporary setback or distraction

- **Supporters**—able to act as a resource, provide necessary information, offer on-the-spot instruction, coordinate efforts of diverse students, and help students to see that they can follow through on their intentions

- **Participants**—able to work or play alongside students to serve as role models and authentic community members; able, as participants rather than bystanders, to learn about the students' perspectives and experiences and become compassionate leaders and supporters

The Educational Approach

A fter working with a workshop group as they collaborated to re-create a traditional festival from Spain, Corey, the workshop counselor,[1] wrote this description of the experience:

Since the Middle Ages, the carpenters of Valencia, Spain, have celebrated the March 19 holiday of St. Joseph with spectacular bonfires and religious processions. For many years carpenters marked the end of winter and celebrated the coming of spring by cleaning their shops and burning large piles of scrap wood in the streets to honor their patron saint. As time passed, the carpenters' woodpiles evolved into elaborate sculptures, or "fallas," made of wood, papier-mâché, and paint. By 1900, the creators of las fallas were spending thousands of hours erecting four- and five-story sculptures, each bearing different human figures and elements expressing a satirical social-commentary theme. Today, the entire festival is known simply as Las Fallas. Each year the many neighborhoods of Valencia spend millions of pesetas constructing their fallas. Competition is stiff, and the hiring of artists, theme selection, and actual construction are all highly guarded secrets until just a few days before the festival, when the fallas are displayed in the major plazas and intersections of Valencia. For several days the city engages in a giant celebration, culminating in the midnight burning of Las Fallas. Nothing is saved, except for el ninot (a small representative figure from the award-winning falla), as the social problems of Spain and Valencia are burned in effigy.

As a counselor in the High/Scope Institute for IDEAS, I led seven teenaged participants in a 20-hour workshop that re-created Las Fallas and adapted it to American society. The workshop was highly successful—for a *variety of reasons. The students not only explored a foreign tradition and learned to create papier-mâché sculptures; they also shared a great sense of achievement after designing and successfully completing such a large-scale undertaking. Most important, however, the students learned a great deal about working cooperatively in a small group, acknowledging the perspectives of others, and problem solving.*

*Key to success in this undertaking were three important features of High/Scope's Institute for adolescents: using the **plan-do-review** model (in which students plan, initiate, and then reflect on, or evaluate, their actions) and employing **divergent questioning**—both in the context of an active learning environment. Also, the students were **engaged as leaders** rather than simply as participants, and this often involved peers helping and teaching one another.*

Introduction and Planning—Heading Off Boredom

The initial introduction and planning stage is extremely important in structuring and setting the overall tone for a workshop. In the case of Las Fallas, introducing the activity presented a couple of problems. First, the Valencian festival is completely unknown to most Americans. Second, if presented in a lecture format, the festival's background information can seem both lengthy and dry. Once Las Fallas is explained, however, the potential for group engagement is enormous. So the first obstacle was figuring out how to introduce such a topic without quickly boring a group of teenagers; the solution was an active beginning.

An Active Beginning—The Divergent Questioning Approach

On arrival, group participants encountered a stack of color photos of the 1990 Las Fallas festival. My questions about the photos kindled their interest: "What do you think these pictures might be of? How do specific sculptures make you feel? What do you think they might mean?" Asking these and other open-ended, thought-provoking questions got the students actively involved with Las Fallas. It was a better approach than expecting them to passively absorb a lecture about the festival.

Asking questions that didn't have just one correct answer engaged the students in thoughtful reflection on the topic. Also, the questions were of a general nature and safe to answer, so students didn't have to fear saying the wrong thing. This avoided creating the "testing" atmosphere that prevails in many educational settings. For example, a teacher may have a "correct" answer in mind in asking a question: "What does this picture mean?" The "correct" answer usually comes from one student, who says exactly what the teacher considers to be right: "This picture tells the story of a Spanish peasant being shot by French soldiers." Others, who may not know the one "correct" answer, hesitate to speak. Instead of using such a direct and focused questioning style, I widened the scope of questions to include elements of personal reflection and insight. ("How do you think this sculpture was made? How would you make a sculpture like this?") This gave students opportunities to reflect and think about questions in their own terms.

Using several sequential questions encouraged the students to think about related aspects of the subject matter: "How does this picture make you feel? What elements of the picture make you feel this way? Why do you think they make you feel this way? What, then, do you see as the message of this painting?" The myriad answers resulting from this technique allow more light to be shed on the issue, and an enriched or alternative answer is often reached. The technique challenges students to develop their own thoughts and ideas and provides everyone with a wide range of information, insights, and opinions that otherwise might not have been revealed.

Applying divergent questioning to the Las Fallas workshop served its purpose well. Questions like "What do you think this sculpture might mean?" and "What do you think this might symbolize?" were answered with a barrage of different and interesting responses. Although some responses demonstrated greater depth or cognitive capacities than others, the process itself allowed for strong participation by students who might have been overshadowed in a more traditional, directive setting. Furthermore, the comments and insights of various individuals not only benefited the group but also produced many more questions for the group to answer. While I did have a set of planned issues for discussion, I only guided the group loosely, with questions designed to allow the students themselves to arrive at the important issues and address them.

At this point, the group had discussed and interpreted the various important elements of Las Fallas, based on the photos of the 1990 festival.

Although the group had to rely on me to explain or identify the roles of cer-tain figures in the sculptures, they were forced to connect these figures to the other elements of the falla and then develop an interpretation of their own. For example, one falla depicted a giant gold lantern that had a witch with a TV camera coming out of the lamp, as smoke. Among other things, many surrounding figures were being strangled by videotape. I provided as little factual information as I could concerning the details of the falla and challenged the students to develop their own interpretation during an in-depth period of divergent questioning. In the end, the group determined that this falla represented biased and abusive TV news reporting. They based their interpretation on the role of the witch, the news logo on the camera, and the fact that many naked and innocent-looking figures were being "hurt" by the surrounding videotape. Even though this was not the exact meaning as expressed by the artist, it was very close, and more important, it demonstrated the deep thought that divergent questioning can inspire.

In addition to the individual falla interpretations, the group also identified, on their own, the following group of key elements common to all fallas:

- *Themes—Each falla had a central theme or topic, an issue of importance to Spaniards, dealing with anything from global politics to commentaries on popular culture.*

- *Criticism—Fallas presented issues in a one-sided manner. Each sculpture was, in essence, an opinion statement on a central issue. The criticism was always strong, and the artists spoke with little restraint.*

- *Humor and satire—Fallas all seemed to make fun of certain issues and people. Figures were often distorted and changed in such a way as to humorously highlight the problems.*

The Design Phase—A Sense of Ownership, Participation, and Self-Direction

Another important element of the High/Scope Institute for IDEAS is that students have control over the direction, theme, and nature of their work, as long as projects fall within a given set of parameters. Not only does this position give the teenagers the sense of respect and control that they desper-

ately want and need, but it also forces them to make decisions and take full responsibility for the project's completion and for its success or failure.

In the case of the Las Fallas endeavor, the group began planning their own fallas by thinking about how a similar event might be applied to American society. As possible themes for their fallas, the students brainstormed to draw up a list of all the problem issues they could think of in their home communities and in the world. The group came up with the following list of issues, or themes: drugs, crime, police brutality, racism, sexism, prejudice, censorship, ignorance (lack of education), gangs, unemployment, homelessness, political corruption, and apathy.

After the list was compiled, we discussed various potential issues, narrowing the list to a core group. This decision-making process was filled with spirited discussion about the relative importance of the issues. Students openly expressed their opinions, and many of them offered personal accounts of how certain problems affected their own lives. This discussion became loud and heated at times, with students enthusiastically debating their ideas. Truly engaged in the discussion, they were approaching problems as if they were entirely theirs to wrestle with and solve. A sense of ownership, participation, and self-direction was obvious. Afterwards, several students openly contrasted our discussion with school situations, where similar topics are discussed in a more passive, controlled manner.

The selection process ended with three different groups deadlocked over three different topics—racism, sexism, and political corruption. Divergent questioning was useful in trying to reconcile various sides of the three-way debate: "What might be one way to solve this problem? What kinds of similarities do you see among these issues?" Eventually the group came to their own unique conclusion. They decided to create a falla by working with the three topics as subthemes under the one general theme of attitudes.

It was interesting to note how the group divided itself to represent these three subthemes. Without any intervention on my part, a black male and a white male chose to represent sexism; a black male and a white male selected racism; and a hispanic female, a black female, and a white male decided to represent corruption in politics. Not only did the group divide itself without any apparent racial bias; they also did so with little thought to social pressure. Those who were "buddies" did not stick together; instead, each student acted on his or her own personal interest. This demonstrated *that they were truly engaged, but it also suggested that the Institute experience as a whole had been successful in breaking down social and racial prejudices.*

Designing the actual falla represented another important phase in the workshop process. Once the subthemes had been chosen, a tentative design had to be made that would best represent each subtheme in a satirical manner within the context of American society. Though the students had found it relatively easy to recognize and interpret satire in the photos of previous fallas, they found it much more difficult to create their own satire. More open-ended questions facilitated the process: "What do you think satire might mean? Can you think of something that is satirical? Can you imagine a scene that might represent racism in a satirical way? How would you represent this problem symbolically? What things symbolize racism to you?"

After more than an hour of paper-balling, brainstorming, and sketching, a basic design was finally agreed on. Each group drew their scene from various angles, using as many tentative measurements as possible. Although the entire falla would consist of three different pieces, they would be only minimally separated by a small three-way wall, thus depicting racism, sexism, *and* political corruption *as parts of the central theme,* attitudes. *The group representing* racism *decided to depict a beating scene involving a case of police brutality; it would show four policemen kicking and beating a fallen man. According to the plan, this scene would be quite elaborate, with one policeman suspended in the air as he jumped onto the fallen man's back. Each figure would be approximately four feet tall and in an action pose. The backdrop would consist of a three-dimensional representation of the victim's car.*

The group representing sexism *chose to depict a rapist and his victim as their subjects. A giant statue of the rapist would be standing with one fist punching while the other dragged a kicking and screaming woman by the hair. The rapist would have a ball and chain around his left leg, representing his incarceration.*

The group depicting political corruption *had perhaps the most complicated plan. An enormous red-white-and-blue Uncle Sam would stand with arms held out, the right patting a rich banker on the head, and the left shoving a shabby-looking man in the face. One of Uncle Sam's legs would be firmly planted on the ground while the other stomped on a small box* containing a homeless person. A small shoeshine boy would be polishing Uncle Sam's boot as it crushed the homeless man's box. Finally, as will be explained later, a third arm would jut out from Uncle Sam's stomach.

Construction—Technical, Social, and Psychological Accomplishments

Construction proved to be by far the most time-consuming and physically difficult task. Beginning, as always, with the first step in the plan-do-review process, we began by thinking of different ways to bring life to our designs. This process served as another wonderful problem-solving exercise, forcing students to think through their construction plans in a detailed, step-by-step manner. Several different strategies were derived for construction of the figures and framework. These ranged from using steel pipes to sculpting styrofoam blocks or joining wooden boards to form the skeleton figures. The specific technique, costs, and advantages involved in using each material, as well as the time needed for construction, were all discussed. As I asked questions and offered feedback, the group planned its own course. Questions included "How could you use styrofoam to build these figures? What is one way you can think of to join these pieces? What potential problems can you imagine? How might you calculate the time needed to build the fallas using this technique?" The group finally reached the conclusion that building wooden skeleton figures and then fleshing them out with chicken wire, papier-mâché, and paint was the best strategy, based on these facts: The materials were abundant and inexpensive; as a group, the students had some experience working with wood; burning the wood would be safe and easier on the environment than burning styrofoam or metal; and the wood and papier-mâché technique was exactly the same as the traditional technique employed in Spain.

Once the means of construction had been developed, construction began, presenting the group with many more interesting challenges. The first task, to put specific measurements to their sketches, led to questions about scale models and human-body proportions. All of the groups had figures that were either bigger or smaller than actual size, so this required applying basic math skills: "If the scale model of a man is four feet tall, how long should his car be? If Uncle Sam is ten feet tall, how long should his arms be?" The answer was offered by one of the students: Ratios

Because it did not focus just on teaching students about a festival in Spain, the Las Fallas workshop exemplified the idea of an open framework. Students explored satire, social criticism, woodworking, art, and mathematics throughout the workshop.

would be used to determine proper scale. Students measured objects around them to establish the actual measurements of people, cars, and any other objects to be represented in the falla. Ratios were then used to calculate the specific measurements for the scale models.

An interesting question came up when students determined that the ten-foot figure of the rapist should have a head some 35 inches around. After discovering this, one of the girls shouted satirically, "That rapist ain't got no big head, it's small and empty!" This comment sparked a conversation that drastically affected how the others constructed their figures. What does size represent? How might you use it to make a statement? *The sexism group thought it would be symbolically perfect to make the rapist's head small to represent his lack of thought.*

Not only did this discovery alter the size and shape of the other figures, but it also inspired the students to do more with the figures. Instead of representing the brutal police as men, they turned them into literal pigs in uniform, complete with curly tails and pointed snouts. Uncle Sam's arms were greatly lengthened, and a third arm was added—one that jutted out from his stomach and held a mobile depicting the White House, the Pentagon, and the houses of Congress. It was obvious that through hands-on experiences, the group had come to grasp the satirical nature of Las Fallas, and now they were manipulating it with great success.

The construction phase began with many more questions: "What size wood do we use? How do you make the limbs look natural and not like stick-figures? How does this saw work?" The discovery process continued as the group worked to find ways to make the figures stable and lifelike. Instead of using long, straight pieces of wood, the students quickly discovered that they could cut smaller pieces at angles (to form limb joints) and then fasten them together by using smaller squares of plywood as nailed-on "patches."

The construction process was impressive, not only because of the technical accomplishments but also because of the social and psychological achievements. For several of the students in the group, power tools were alien and scary devices. With a little encouragement and hands-on learning, however, the students quickly overcame both fears and gender stereotypes. Though neither of the female participants had previous construction experience, both quickly became such productive and competent participants that many of the boys came to them for help or support.

Completion of the wooden skeletons was a great boost for the group; seeing some tangible results of their work inspired them to push ahead. The planning phase had been active and engaging, but it lacked the physical sense of accomplishment that construction provided. Once the skeletons had been made, the figures had to be covered with chicken wire and papier-mâché. Again the group had to wrestle with new technical questions. Although I knew good answers to their problems, I maintained my role as facilitator, allowing them to solve problems themselves without too much struggling. They quickly discovered that teamwork was the fastest and most efficient means of chicken-wiring the figures. One person cut the chicken wire while another stapled it to the frames and dictated the measurements for the next piece.

The papier-mâché phase of the project proved to be the messiest and hardest. All the completed chicken-wire figures had to be covered with papier-mâché. Hands, facial features, and heads also had to be made. The students were resistant to the mess that the flour paste made and also were frustrated by the required attention to detail. Balloons were chosen for heads, and hands were made from blocks of wood and dowel pieces. Slowly but surely they covered each figure with papier-mâché and painted it in bright colors.

After all the arduous work put in by the group, it struck me that perhaps they would hesitate to follow through with the burning of the sculptures; they seemed to have such a deep sense of ownership over their *creations. However, I was wrong. In fact, they had already begun planning the dramatic event—everything including the site for the festival, the speeches they would present, and the safety issues related to the burning.*

The Conclusion—Sharing Insights and Accomplishments

The group's efforts were fully rewarded one evening, when the entire Institute community was brought together in the valley and the Las Fallas creation was unveiled. Each student in the workshop spoke proudly of the sculptures, describing the creative processes involved and the political and social implications. From the looks on the faces in the crowd, it was clear that the presentation had an emotional impact on everyone present—students, staff, and directors. Finally, after everyone had a chance to tour the sculptures and digest their meaning, each artist approached the work and removed a small piece as a token of remembrance. Then came the flames, and the powerful insights of seven teenagers burned their way into the memories of all present.

• • •

The Las Fallas workshop described in the opening vignette offers a fine illustration of the High/Scope educational approach, which the Institute provides as a guide to all staff members. The approach asks staff to create an active learning environment, using a given topic as an organizing factor rather than as the exclusive goal or focus of attention. It asks staff to create a framework—what we refer to as an *open framework*—that will allow students and staff members to work together to determine the course of events within the workshop, work project, or club. It asks staff to take an active but supportive role, sharing planning, initiation, and evaluation with the participants.

An open framework allows individuals to work at different levels of expertise and to identify their own goals and tasks within the larger, group goals. Instead of requiring all students to achieve the same knowledge or understanding of a topic, it allows individuals to gain different things from the group experience.

The Las Fallas workshop exemplifies an open framework because it did not focus exclusively on teaching students about the festival. It was designed to also offer them opportunities to learn a whole range of new concepts and skills: how to create satire and social criticism, how to work with tools, how to solve the artistic and physical problems presented, how to design sculptures and then evaluate materials for realizing those designs, how to use math concepts to work to scale, how to function effectively in teams and small groups.

The Las Fallas workshop counselor, Corey, had a pleasing, low-key style that works well with young people. But the success of the workshop was not just a result of his natural teaching talent; it sprang also from the design of the workshop, which Corey based on the training he had received in using the High/Scope educational approach.

At the Institute, staff-in-training are asked to plan instructional program times step-by-step, with the goal of facilitating active learning in each phase of their plan. The educational approach calls for a style of teaching (and learning) that supports each individual student in her or his own development. This means that instructors can expect their various students to learn different things, respond to ideas individually, need different kinds of support, and integrate the learning in unique ways. Instructors using the approach are available to provide or coordinate this support, because the open-framework design, use of concrete materials, and active collaboration of the students frees instructors from many of the constraints they would experience in a traditional classroom setting.

Although the students in the Las Fallas workshop were focused as a group on the creation of a falla, each of them experienced that activity differently. For the two girls, overcoming their uneasiness with power tools and becoming skilled enough to act as resources was one outcome of the workshop. For another student, understanding the mathematical work with ratios was a breakthrough. For yet another student, the expression of social concerns in an artistic way and the new understandings of satire and irony made a big impression.

Many of the positive aspects of the Las Fallas experience have lasting effects that cannot be measured: the opportunity for positive interracial, mixed-gender interaction; the inspiration of Corey as a near-peer; the fun of making something so concrete; the glimpse into a different culture and its practices.

What students take away from a month of this style of learning is not a transcript of subjects covered. Instead it is personal development, intellectual and emotional growth, greater maturity, increased self-confidence, new ideas about what is possible, greater excitement about learning and exploration, greater breadth, multiple experiences with groups, and more. In some cases a student will go home inspired by a particular topic, anxious to explore it academically. In many cases, students go home with greater awareness about how to take responsibility for themselves and how to work more effectively with others.

Although these outcomes may seem vague or general, the instructional settings at the Institute are just the opposite. They are grounded in concrete experiences, specific actions or activities, and tangible products or performances.

The educational approach can be summarized as follows:

1. Balancing teacher-initiated and student-initiated learning within an open framework

2. Incorporating the five essential components of *choice, active learning, plan-do-review, cooperative learning,* and *opportunities for leadership*

3. Using the following strategies that support students in their active learning:

   - Create multi-ability learning situations.

   - Divide activities into manageable stages.

   - Help students to identify tangible products and goals.

   - Use an open-ended questioning style and a nondirective style of teaching, which keeps learning centered on the students and their group process.

   - Engage students actively in each stage of the process.

   - Engineer for success.

   - Encourage students to teach and learn from one another.

   - Create learning opportunities within the context of active explorations.

Each of these elements of the educational approach will be described further.

Balancing Teacher-Initiated and Student-Initiated Learning Within an Open Framework

Learning at the Institute is neither student-centered nor teacher-centered. As just described, instructors create an open framework into which both students and teachers have ongoing creative input. The framework is created first by the instructor's planning. Corey, for example, determined a topic for exploration—Las Fallas—and a format for exploring it. He prepared materials that would stimulate participation and interaction and tried to predict a rough sequence of events. Then the students—through their discussion, responses to the materials, and group planning—further determined the form and focus of the workshop. As the work got under way, a discussion ensued in which Corey and the students posed questions to one another, proposed possible answers, taught one another skills, identified problems and solutions, and evaluated results.

Corey was neither too passive nor too active. Instead, he adopted an active role in stimulating thoughtful actions and designs. He taught some skills and techniques. He occasionally helped the group to refocus their attention and stay on track. Frequently he stood back and allowed students to grapple with problems and come up with their own solutions.

The students also took responsibility for how the work unfolded and what their own individual contributions might be. As skills, enthusiasm, and group consensus dictated, the leadership of the group shifted from one individual to another.

This balance of student and teacher input allows all individuals to make contributions and to feel that they have a stake in what happens during the course of a workshop. Students learn to collaborate on setting group goals, but they are helped by instructors and peers to find individual ways to contribute, ways that do not involve just giving in to the will of the majority.

The activity itself, when well selected and designed, offers a natural framework. The Las Fallas festival includes within its tradition the building of satirical figures; thus students were given this traditional activity as a basis for their planning. They did not have to design a festival from the ground up, though they were free to choose to do so within the open framework of the workshop.

The High/Scope educational approach asks teachers to think about how to *frame* an activity so it offers a good balance of student and teacher initiation and participation. This open framework is then given greater shape as the instructor incorporates the five key elements of learning.

Incorporating the Five Essential Components

The five essential components of High/Scope's approach to learning (and teaching) are as follows: choice, active learning, plan-do-review, cooperative learning, and opportunities for leadership. Because these components are so crucial, it is useful to look at them more closely and to discuss them in the context of the Las Fallas workshop.

Choice

All of the participants of the Las Fallas workshop began the workshop as a result of an individual choice. They each selected this workshop out of a list of nine offerings, agreeing to be active contributors and to explore this topic over the duration of the 10 sessions it spanned. Because every instructional topic at the Institute is elective and each instructional situation contains plentiful choices, students tend to be interested and motivated—or are willing to become motivated. Beginning a workshop with a hands-on activity almost invariably motivates and draws in students whose interest has not yet been fully engaged.

Within each instructional setting, students make choices about how to structure their tasks, what roles they want to play in group endeavors, how to focus their efforts, which materials and processes they will use. All of these choices allow students to repeatedly discover and act on their own motivations. They find they can shape learning situations to fit their own interests.

In the Las Fallas workshop, Corey began with some photos that he hoped would stimulate interest and discussion. He neither directed the discussion nor questioned students to elicit specific "correct" responses (the "guess what I'm thinking game" that students sometimes encounter in classroom situations). The students knew they were free to respond to his questions with their own interpretations and ideas.

As an instructor, Corey did have some key issues in mind that he hoped students would come up with, but he was also ready to abandon his expectations to follow the students' lead. Some teachers find this stance difficult—having one's own ideas ready as a backup but at the same time being willing to let the students' activity evolve in its own direction.

Corey needed to carefully think through the parameters of the open-framework exploration before he introduced the activity. If the activity had been introduced in a way that was too vague or abstract, students could easily have gotten lost in listing the ills of modern society, and they would not

At the Institute, students' choices are not limited to selecting which activity to participate in. These students, who have selected a photography workshop, can also decide how to structure their tasks, what role they want to play in group endeavors, how to focus their efforts, and which materials and processes they will use.

have gotten around to creating a falla to represent their opinions. If he tried to make the discussion too specific—for example, centering on practices in Spain—he might have excluded those students who would have rightly felt they had nothing to contribute, since they had never been to Spain.

Corey's job throughout the workshop was to provide a framework for action, strategies for proceeding, and necessary information when asked by students. As he put it, "The group was given complete control over the direction, theme, and nature of their falla, as long as the project fell within a given set of parameters." He saw his role as helping the students identify or create those parameters in a way that would allow them to proceed successfully. Once they accomplished that early in the workshop, the project truly became theirs to direct and shape.

Because students at the Institute perceive their choices as real, and because the ongoing options engage students in individualized ways, many participants tend to behave far more responsibly than they are used to behaving in school. We believe there is a strong link between choice and personal responsibility: When students feel they are free to define the ways they participate, they are almost always willing to participate. Truancy is nearly nonexistent at the Institute, and tardiness is a result of someone getting deeply engaged in an activity and losing track of time more often than it is a statement of resistance or rebellion.

Choice becomes a way to reengage students' interest at each phase of a workshop. Once the group had agreed on themes in the Las Fallas workshop, for example, Corey once again introduced choice in a problem-solving form by posing the following questions: How will we make these fallas? What materials will work best? Who will do which task? What techniques will allow us to work together efficiently to get the job done?

These questions are asked repeatedly throughout the Institute session. As time goes on, students learn to pose these questions themselves, continually pausing to look at their options. The process of considering their choices, generating options, and creating a plan of action is one of the most valuable learning habits students take away from the Institute. Being aware that they *have* choices gives them a greater stake in what and how they learn.

Active Learning

Although many programs for teenagers advertise "active learning," how that term is defined varies widely. At High/Scope, active learning means using materials, tools, and processes. It means that young people learn using their bodies—their hands as well as their minds, their physical as well as their creative talents. An active learning approach to math, for example, might involve building a suspension bridge or designing a sculpture. An active learning approach to drama might involve exploring human reactions in a drama workshop that culminates in creating and producing an original play.

As Corey planned his workshop, his challenge was to find natural ways to make it active. Since his goal was not to teach about festivals in Spain but rather to help students experience the artistic and social expression that is typified by this festival, his job was a bit easier. The natural, active way for students to learn about Las Fallas was to recreate the festival on their own terms.

Some topics lend themselves to activity and use of materials, tools, and processes; some do not. Thus there is an emphasis at the Institute on ideas that can be applied, usually in interdisciplinary ways, and on subject matter that is multifaceted and can be learned through doing.

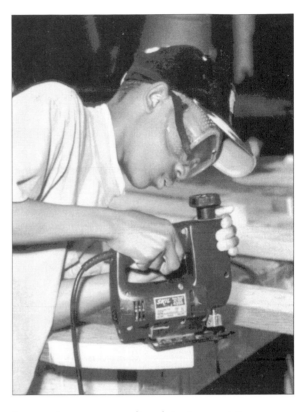

For many teenagers, grounding abstract concepts in concrete action is a necessary part of learning. High/Scope's educational approach allows for many different learning styles within each instructional situation.

We do not condemn writing, reading, and other more abstract, less physical pursuits. They too have a place in the learning and development of young minds. But too often that is the exclusive learning mode available to young people—when developmentally they are bursting with energy, needing to move, to explore, to participate in events, and to discover that they are competent doers. The Institute's emphasis, once again, reflects High/Scope's goal to expose participants to experiences they might not have in traditional academic settings.

Active learning makes some concepts more meaningful to students. The creation of a falla, for example, takes this festival out of the abstract realm and makes it a meaningful process that gives many of the students a greater insight into the people who created it. For some students, grounding abstract concepts in concrete action is a necessary part of learning. High/Scope's educational approach makes room for many different learning styles within each instructional situation; styles range from verbal to graphic, from abstract to concrete.

In the early part of the Las Fallas workshop, Corey incorporated discussions inspired initially by photographs. This was a somewhat risky beginning, because discussions can easily degenerate into a dialogue between one verbal student and the instructor, or into a monologue (the instructor's) that strives valiantly to spark a response in dull, blank faces. Corey was able to elicit active participation because of the following factors: (1) The students wanted to explore Las Fallas. (2) The discussions were based on evocative (and concrete) photos. (3) The students were asked about their personal views and feelings, not about abstract topics outside their experience. (4) The purpose of the discussion, clear to all the students, was to plan and prepare for the activity of making a falla. Discussion that is purposeful and based on personal knowledge invites active participation by all.

Instruction at the Institute is organized around the use of materials and tools that are stimulating to learners. Put teenagers in a room full of stage props, art materials, shop tools, musical instruments, or electronic equipment, and you are far more likely to see a flicker of interest than if you place them at desks with textbooks. Although there is nothing wrong with textbooks—they can be great resources for information— there is something definitely *right* about including the use of materials, tools, and interactive processes in a learning setting.

Most of the Las Fallas workshop was taken up with the tasks of manually creating what the group had envisioned. During this time, students were learning to solve the problems inherent in working with wood, tools, chicken wire, and papier-mâché; beyond that, they learned to collaborate, to see a vision through to realization, and to use new tools and processes. As a social studies lesson, it was somewhat slow—in 20 hours of interaction they only "covered" one festival. As a lesson in artistic and social expression, however, it was more adequate. And as an experience in building group cohesion and pride in self-expression, it was rich and successful. Active learning offers students a chance to develop far greater breadth, investment, and emotional-intellectual integration than an abstract discussion or paper-and-pencil activity can provide.

Some teachers fear that in a traditional school setting, an active learning approach would not allow them to cover all the information they are required to cover within a given period of time. While this is a realistic fear, many classroom teachers have found ways to make the required curriculum active and to incorporate choice, cooperation, and the other elements of High/Scope's approach within the academic setting.

Active learning is also *purposeful learning.* A gardening project can be active, in that students are using tools and physical skills, but it is *active learning* only if it uses the context of gardening to help students to explore and apply other concepts as well. If students take time to plan their garden aesthetically, research the requirements for each plant to flourish, learn to evaluate and enrich the quality of the soil, learn the engineering and construction skills involved in landscaping, and create a system for effective water-distribution, then they are engaging in active learning.

Students who are exposed to problem solving and exploration through purposeful active learning experiences are developing the skills and inclination to contribute to their community in concrete ways.

Students who are exposed to the problem solving, exploration, and expression engendered by active learning are likely to be active members of their families and of the larger community. If students have experience in seeing a problem and creating a process for addressing it with action, then we believe they are developing the imagination, skills, and inclination to contribute and provide service in concrete ways to their community.

Plan-Do-Review

Plan-do-review is a process by which young people become aware of what they are doing and intentional in their actions. Because they are at an age when they are becoming increasingly able to reflect on experiences and to have insight into how they would like to do things, plan-do-review is a particularly appropriate process for teenagers.

It is amazing how such a simple formula can have a profound effect on the quality of an experience. When students take time to think through what they intend to do (*plan*), then carry out their actions with plans and hypotheses in mind (*do*), and then review what they have done by evaluating and representing it to others (*review*), a deep engagement takes place.

Engaging teenagers in planning encourages them to become aware of their thinking processes and development and to take responsibility for the outcomes of their work.

Corey used the plan-do-review process repeatedly throughout the course of the workshop. He asked participants to brainstorm, create plans and designs for their themes, and pull together a blueprint for the overall falla. Students then referred to these designs throughout the week, discussing what they had originally envisioned and how that was changing as they got into the details of making the figures.

While executing their plans, students discovered (once again) that making something requires mastering tools, gaining skill with their hands, getting dirty, and struggling with materials. They needed to stop periodically to reflect on what they were doing and how it worked. This offered them many opportunities to identify and solve problems, to deepen their understanding of the purpose of Las Fallas, to adjust or learn new techniques, to turn to peers for help, to rethink their intentions, to discuss the requirements of the various steps of the process, and to reorganize their efforts. They took time to congratulate themselves and one another on their accomplishments and to let the excitement of what they were achieving truly sink in. This excitement communicated itself to the entire Institute community, who anxiously awaited the unveiling of the falla and the ritual burning ceremony in which they all took part.

When staff members use plan-do-review as an instructional tool, it challenges young people to develop their capacity for information processing, problem solving, self-awareness, initiative, and responsibility. Each step of the plan-do-review process strengthens these capacities.

Plan. Students become aware of and take responsibility for their thinking processes and development. They are encouraged to analyze situations and goals; to consider a variety of resources; and to be open to new approaches, alternatives, solutions, and directions. For adolescents, planning is generally detailed and often involves the design and creation of models.

Do. Students make choices, propose initiatives, test different approaches, and carry out plans. They are encouraged to take risks and to persist in the tasks they designed, even when faced with obstacles. The work of carrying out plans is always active and frequently alters students' perceptions and deepens their understanding of what they are doing.

Review. Students reflect on the effectiveness of their actions both in regard to their own objectives and in regard to the impact of their actions on others. They also consider revisions to original ideas or plans that would have resulted in more-desirable outcomes. The review process occurs intermittently as a project progresses and often causes students to modify their plans or their understanding of what they are trying to do. On completion of projects, the review includes an evaluation of what was tried and how it worked out and a representation of the project to others in the community, through performance, presentation, or other creative modes.

Cooperative Learning

We believe that teenagers have as much to learn from their peers as they do from adults. We are also convinced that the opportunities to develop self-confidence increase exponentially when students are collaborating and helping one another rather than competing.

Corey designed his workshop, for example, so students would need to work together, sharing skills as well as ideas and acting independently of his leadership. Seeing peers as resources and observing other students' talents and skills help students to build respect for one another. As it worked out, the collaboration that happened in the Las Fallas workshop also provided wonderful mixed-gender, mixed-racial groupings that stemmed naturally from students' shared interests.

It is not often that teenagers have opportunities to collaborate in significant ways. In most traditional high school settings, students each have their own work to do, and helping others is considered cheating. When students are pushed to compete with one another for grades, they are less likely to see peers as resources and to define their own personal goals or ideas of fulfillment.

The High/Scope educational approach suggests that staff structure each program offering as a group, or collaborative, experience. Students exploring techniques for using tools in the shop, for example, are encouraged to take time to teach one another what they have discovered. They are then further encouraged to come up with ideas for developing some group products and to figure out how to break the process down into tasks that enable each individual to contribute in a way that is comfortable for him or her.

It is exhilarating and meaningful for teenagers to arrive at a group understanding, a group product, or a collective presentation and to feel they have each contributed to the outcome. Over and over again, we hear Institute students saying proudly:

I helped to build that bridge!

• • •

This was my idea, then she suggested that, then we
all just somehow realized it should look this way.

• • •

We tried our first idea, but it didn't work, so then Jill
suggested we try this other thing, and Marla added
the suggestion that we use more music, and Tom
and Jerome went and found an oscillator, and then it
just developed from there . . .

This is the language of engagement, of awareness of process in
which students have repeated opportunities for group planning,
group decision-making, collaborative investigation, and creation of
group products and performances. It is a context that allows beginners and more-advanced students to work together and to learn from
each other. It is a context in which the benefits of brainstorming, of
combining talents and perspectives, of articulating opinions, of
thinking things through, have their natural place.

Helping young people to collaborate successfully is an art
form. Too often their experiences of working in groups have led to
failure. They were asked to produce something as a group, then were
abandoned to the task. As a result, one or two students did the work,
while the others stood around confused.

Corey worked hard to make sure that his group could accomplish what it set out to do. Yet much of his hard work was not
evident to the students. He had mastered the art of how to effectively
facilitate the group experience without dominating it. He provided
them with an initial shared experience, so each participant had a
basis for contributing; he asked students open-ended questions (in a
friendly, low-key style) to help them become more aware of what
they were doing and why; and then he was able to help the students
break the process down into tasks that various individuals could
undertake.

As part of a learning and working context, collaboration makes
sense for several reasons. Because teenagers are increasingly concerned with their membership in groups and their community, it is
developmentally appropriate for them to have purposeful and meaningful interactions. Because adolescents of any age can vary widely

In the High/Scope approach, staff structure activities as collaborative experiences. Students are encouraged to teach one another what they have learned.

in levels of understanding, emotional maturity, physical size, and comfort with abstraction, it makes sense to structure their interactive learning experiences to accommodate a wide range of skills and styles of participation.

Collaboration on projects—on writing and producing a drama, on designing and building an instrument to measure a river's flow—gives young people a sense of intimacy and connection with their peers. Getting to know someone in the context of interdependent activity allows students to form bonds that are unusual for many of them, bonds that help break down barriers based on prejudice or status.

A final reason why collaboration makes sense is that it teaches teenagers skills that are extremely valuable to employers and to society as a whole. When young people are given plentiful opportunities to work with others to define needs, to identify and address problems, to create group products, and to communicate the process to others, they become better citizens and employees, more able to work on a team, more aware of the needs and perspectives of people around them, and more likely to engage in service to others.

Leadership Development

Corey's description of his workshop makes no mention of any particular student becoming the leader. That is because, within the workshop's 20 hours, *each* of the students found chances to lead (and follow) in a comfortable give-and-take fashion. The two girls who had never used power tools before mastered them so well that they were sought out as resources by their peers; in a sense, they were leaders. But by the same token, the person who thought of integrating three themes into one, the person who figured out how to more effectively use chicken wire, and the students who helped motivate the whole group to finish the papier-mâché stage were also leaders.

When an adult refrains from assuming a dominant role and instead becomes a facilitator, multiple opportunities emerge for students to take on leadership. When an activity is broken down into stages, with steps, and when students are conscious of the process they are following, then more of them are likely to lead at various junctures. The most articulate students do not automatically dominate the process, since many of the stages require actions. Likewise, the more active students also do not dominate, because many steps require verbalization and reflection. The older students might lead from time to time, but when a group breaks down into pairs or triads, it is just as likely that a younger student might take on leadership or provide extra motivation for a particular task.

Corey designed the Las Fallas workshop so it would feel like a group accomplishment from start to finish. In the planning stages, one or two students actually organized suggestions into a written list. Another student sketched a plan with help from yet another, who was not comfortable sketching but had plenty of opinions to share. In the actual building of the falla, each student had a task and needed to coordinate with peers to accomplish it. During the reflection process, each student was asked for ideas and offered them. The whole group presented the finished product to the Institute community.

Leadership is the ability to positively influence and guide a group. In their school settings, many of the Institute participants do not get a chance to see themselves as leaders. That role is often reserved for the teachers and the academically gifted or socially adept students. While some of the Institute students are naturally outgoing and able to influence others, others have often been seen as disruptive troublemakers rather than strong, positive leaders in their regular school settings.

At the Institute, however, all students have an opportunity to rethink their participation in groups and in the community. Their understanding of their role shifts when they are interacting in purposeful settings. Measuring and cutting the wood, mixing paste to the right consistency, determining the proper placement of figures in a falla—these create a learning context that thoroughly changes the ways students interact with one another. Students discover new strengths in themselves and in others, which leads them to have greater self-respect and appreciation of others.

The group setting also allows students to practice leading in concrete, practical ways. Staff are trained to vary the learning activities and to set them up in such a way that diverse opportunities for leadership are constantly arising— opportunities that call on the strengths of the various individuals in a group.

In this way, leadership is learned in the context of group cooperation, not in isolation or as an exercise in exerting control. A leader one moment is a follower the next. Because of this, there is rarely a problem with one student dominating or intimidating the others. Instead, a growing mutual respect arises over the course of the month as students take turns initiating and following, leading and being led, in a constant communal exchange. In the account that follows, Institute staff member Jim Brunberg[2] describes the communal exchange that took place during planning and implementation of one of his workshops.

●　●　●

A Stained Glass Workshop

Given the technically frustrating and sometimes unpredictable intricacies of working with glass, working with six students doing stained glass projects over the course of a 20-hour workshop proved to be quite a challenge. The skills required to complete a stained glass project are diverse and not easily perfected. Because trial and error can be costly and even dangerous, certain specific rules apply to successful glass handling and cutting. Still, as is common during the High/Scope Institute, I proposed lofty goals for these students as learners, collaborators, leaders, and artists. The goals were equally lofty for myself as a role model, mentor, and educator. In the end, this workshop surpassed my high expectations. My initial goals, as well as many others I hadn't anticipated, were met.

Goal Setting

Beginning stained glass artists start, in most cases, by piecing together a few simple shapes into a two-dimensional design suitable for hanging on a wall or in a window. Although the more complex three-dimensional plans often end in frustration, I was confident that each of the students had the potential to complete such a project. Thus, the goal I projected was that each student make a stained glass item that was useful and three-dimensional, for example, a lamp.

The students were informed right away that a major purpose of the workshop was to develop tactile skills, both general ones and ones specific to this craft. The list of skills, which we decided to post on the wall, included the following: cutting glass both straight and in curves, tapping glass, grinding glass, pattern design, pattern cutting, and wrapping glass with solder.

Another, less product-oriented goal was to have students teach these skills to one another over the course of the sessions. This was a key issue that greatly affected my planning of the workshop. My goal was actually twofold: to have every student teach one of the skills at some point and to have every student learn a majority of the skills from another student. As the workshop unfolded, the students' varying rates of progress and differing luck with the tools proved extremely conducive to this give-and-take learning process.

The peer-instruction strategy was an integral part of the workshop. Students quickly acquired the necessary skills and mastered them to a teachable level, so the idea worked very well.

The Instructional Approach

In addition to peer instruction, several other important strategies contributed to the workshop's success. The most important were offering choice, providing for active learning, incorporating the plan-do-review process, and using an open-ended questioning style.

__Offering choice.__ "Think of the largest thing you know of made of stained glass. Then think of the smallest thing you can imagine making out of stained glass. Then list five project ideas that might fit into a 20-hour workshop." This is the type of brainstorming I proposed to the students after an initial glass-cutting exercise in which they familiarized themselves with some of the limitations of working with glass. I also littered *the table with magazines about stained glass and sketches from past project plans. In this initial brainstorming session, my goal was to keep their field of choice as wide open as possible and at the same time to avoid the "blank-page" anxiety that often accompanies open-ended projects.*

As students became more familiar with project parameters, including the time-consuming nature of working with glass, they narrowed down their lists of proposed projects. One student abandoned his list entirely, suddenly inspired by an urge to create an abstract zucchini sculpture that would light up from the inside! Each student ended up choosing and independently designing his or her own realistic but challenging stained glass item. As students drew plans for their creations, I encouraged them to check fellow students' designs for practicality in terms of shapes of glass (angles, curve radii, size and number of pieces, etc.). No two projects were alike or even closely related. What developed were six extremely artistic endeavors.

***Providing for active learning.** Working with stained glass is by nature a hands-on activity. It necessitates the physical application of several skills and academic concepts. To engage and stimulate students to learn, an active beginning is especially important; so I had students safely cutting and breaking glass within the first few minutes of the workshop. This functioned well as a brief lesson in the limitations of working with glass, but more important, it allowed students to put their hands and minds to work immediately and independently.*

***Incorporating plan-do-review.** Planning and reviewing played extremely important roles in the stained glass workshop. Development of plans, described in more detail in the session-by- session part of this narrative, was a process that required creativity, technical expertise, mathematical skills, and ability to foresee possible obstacles and outcomes. Students worked both in pairs and individually, seeking out feedback from me and their peers on various stages of their plans. Planning did not by any means end when work began. Planning was an ongoing process that took place at varying levels. As a group, we spent time each day planning the two-hour work session; as individuals, students planned the pace of their own projects. Planning the final presentations of the results to other students at the Institute was a group effort.*

Ongoing reflection, or review, is a process that parallels planning. As the workshop proceeded, the group worked together to add to the list of gen-

eral and specific skills they were learning (for example, squaring, measuring angles). Halfway through the workshop, we demonstrated for the whole Institute the skills we had learned so far and presented the unfinished projects. Some students demonstrated glass cutting, to show others the degree of difficulty of the craft. The students took tremendous pride in their projects and were anxious to show them off.

I implemented the plan-do-review process often when working with students on an individual basis. Students were asked to compare their initial sketches to their product, both during and at the end of the work process. Having the freedom to change their plans allowed students to think creatively and to pose constant challenges to themselves.

Using an open-ended questioning style. Asking open-ended questions of students engages them in the learning process and allows them to put answers in their own words and come up with their own examples. Another important aspect of the questioning style is considering how to respond to students' questions in a way that will allow them to arrive at the answer themselves. During the workshop, students commonly asked, "How do I do this?" I usually answered, "Let's go see if [another student] has figured that out." My frequent question to students was "Will this work?" I tried to ask this in all kinds of situations, not only potentially problematic ones. Usually, this question led to a student-sponsored review of our discoveries so far of the properties of glass-working, then further questioning and a redirection of the skill being attempted.

Academic Concepts

Although working with stained glass is certainly an art, helping teenagers to develop the skills involved meant exploring a wide range of academic concepts. Specifically, the workshop touched on concepts from geometry, physics, and chemistry. Each concept was introduced to the whole group through hands-on exploration and discussion, but more important, each concept surfaced again with individuals as it became directly applicable to success in their respective projects. At the end of each day's session, the group reviewed its progress and reflected on new concepts that had arisen.

In terms of geometry, I insisted that students plan the exact angles at which the major components of their creations would join. Most of the students admitted to having no previous experience with measuring angles or calculating distance using the Pythagorean Theorem. Also, in our preliminary cutting practice on scrap glass, we tried as a group to establish the smallest angle that can consistently be cut in glass. We performed a similar study of curve-cutting possibilities; this involved mathematically determining the radii of curves.

In an important introductory session, we explored the light spectrum and color concepts as they related to our work. This process included solidifying the students' grasp of such terms as transparent, opaque, translucent, and primary colors.

Once students in the stained glass workshop had experimented with glass cutting, they were aware of the challenges associated with cutting different shapes and could then move into planning their designs.

To learn how to use the flux, how to foil the glass, and how to use the soldering gun, students needed to understand something about oxidation of metal, melting temperature, and heat expansion. These scientific principles were approached in an exploratory manner. As the students' projects progressed, questions invariably arose concerning the behavior of the glass, foil, leading, flux, and tools. I facilitated one-on-one scientific inquiries into the questions and later asked students to share their understanding of the principles with others who were newly encountering the same questions.

Narrative of Events

Session 1: The group gathered around a table covered with tools, glass, and sources of project ideas. My first question to them addressed difficulties they might expect to have when cutting glass. We brainstormed about ways to minimize these difficulties and cut safely. After the group broke into pairs and prepared glass-cutting areas, I modeled cutting straight lines only and then had them practice for 15 minutes with partners. One pair quickly mastered the straight-cutting, so at their table, I showed them how to cut a few kinds of curves. A few minutes later, they instructed the others on curve-cutting. After this, I told them to cut until they felt comfortable with the glass and familiar with its limitations. Once they felt they were ready, they came to me individually, demonstrated use of the cutting and shaping tools, and started on planning patterns.

Sessions 2 and 3: The next two sessions consisted of drawing patterns and then checking, revising, and cutting them out. These sessions were devoted to the many specifics that need to be considered in designing and planning a stained glass project. One student decided to undertake a somewhat unorthodox project that consisted of building on the glass pieces layer by layer, rather than cutting, foiling, and soldering them in the usual order. I wholeheartedly supported his vision: to create a stained glass zucchini sculpture that would light up from the inside. Although the pace of his project was different from that of the rest of the group, it worked out well, because he learned the foiling and soldering skills early enough to have mastered them by the time the other projects reached these stages. This meant he was able to teach these skills very effectively to the others.

Session 4: Students continued to move from drawing plans to cutting out their plans and then into cutting the glass itself. One student had taken on a difficult lamp project, with a design requiring many curved cuts. I started to worry but did not intervene, because his passion and working pace led me to believe that he might finish the project. All other students continued to work without frustration.

Session 5: When he encountered an unfriendly piece of glass and couldn't get it to break properly, the lamp-maker lost his patience and decided that his project was too difficult. He wanted to rip up his original plans and discard the glass he had cut so far. After catching his aborted project pieces, literally, on their way into the trash, I called for a group meeting. As a group, the students helped him sketch out an idea for a simplified version of the lamp. By this point, the zucchini sculpture had become three-dimensional, and two other projects were ready to begin soldering.

Sessions 6 and 7: During these sessions, all projects but the lamp moved into the soldering stage. At this point, we experienced a back-up of students waiting for the soldering iron, which could only be shared by two *students at a time. Meanwhile, one student taught the newcomers how to solder by giving them hands-on experience with her project, a map of Africa. The waiting students designed frames or suspension systems for their projects, as well. But most important, two of the waiting students helped the lamp-maker grind and foil-wrap his glass pieces, so he could finish the lamp by the end of the workshop.*

Sessions 8 and 9: The back-up continued at the soldering station, so the lamp-maker caught up with the others as they designed frames for their projects, boxes for bringing them home, methods of hanging them, and ways of presenting them at the evening program. By performance time, everybody had a completed work of glass, although many of the joints still needed more solder or smoothing. These details were handled by the students in their free time. The presentation was vibrant and ecstatic. Everyone seemed to have fun and surpassed their own expectations as well as mine. Even the lamp-maker attributed his need for revision not to a failure of any kind, but to hasty planning. The six completed projects were a three-dimensional butterfly sculpture to be set on a table near a window; two large window hangings (one of Africa, one an array of geometrical shapes); a large candle shield that held candles at different heights for interesting effects; a large lamp with four sides; and of course the zucchini sculpture.

• • •

Using Strategies That Support Students

Both Corey Shouse and Jim Brunberg described how, in conducting their workshops, they "engineered for success." Their staff training for the Institute taught them how to plan their workshops in such a way that each student could experience success in individual terms. Their training in the High/Scope educational approach incorporated the following support strategies:

Create Multi-ability Learning Situations

Suppose that a staff member wants to conduct a workshop to teach guitar playing. Using the traditional method of teaching guitar—introducing specific chords in a sequenced set of lessons—does not fit the High/Scope model. Instead, the first task is to look at how guitar can be taught in the context of a student-centered, exploratory activity suited to various ability levels. To do this, the staff member needs to identify some educational goals that relate to (1) exposure to new processes and ideas, (2) experience with specific tools and activities of the field, and (3) application of concepts in a variety of creative and intellectually challenging contexts. For example, the staff member may decide that an appropriate working goal would be "writing our own music, using the guitar as an instrument." This shifts the focus from a goal of acquiring skill to a context, or activity, goal.

The staff member might decide to relate the goal to the ongoing Institute culture by asking workshop participants to identify a purpose for writing their music: to use as background for a dramatic presentation, to perform at the musicale, to use as the introduction to a video. In some cases, depending on the time available, individual students might choose diverse goals: One might write for the musicale, two others might put together music for an art show, yet another group might decide to do mood music for an evening program. In other cases, especially when time is limited, the staff member might preselect the context and advertise it as part of the activity.

Once the activity is designed to be an exploration within a context, it can be set up to accommodate different levels of skill and understanding. Staff are asked to think through what kinds of concrete experiences they can provide that will accommodate beginners, students with some experience, and students who are already quite skilled. This is often accomplished with the use of *exploration* (seeing how many different kinds of sounds can be made with guitars); *peer teaching* (two students who already play guitar acting as resources, and the others deciding how they want to use their talents in the production); and *breaking into small affinity groups* (students who want to write songs to sing meeting together, students who want to write mood music meeting together, and students who want to create their own guitar style meeting together).

Divide Activities Into Manageable Stages

Most teachers plan their instruction with a beginning, a middle, and an end. The High/Scope approach uses a variation of this pattern.

Staff try to start each workshop (or club or project) with a *participatory group activity*—something to give students a concrete basis for further planning, exploration, and goal setting. In the guitar workshop, for example, it might be a 10- to 15-minute exploration and brainstorming activity to see how many kinds of sounds can be made with the guitars. In the stained glass workshop, Jim used an initial glass-cutting activity to give students a real sense of what glass cutting entails. In the Las Fallas workshop, Corey took a risk, as was mentioned, by starting with students' responses to photographs. A gardening project might start with 10 minutes of experimentation with several garden tools. In a drama workshop, the students might be given 10 minutes to improvise about finding themselves in a certain setting. The initial activity should be structured so it

- Allows each person to experience success

- Provides materials sufficient for all students to participate

- Is enjoyable

- Allows for individual choice

- Accommodates different levels of understanding and physical ability

- Is imaginative, free from pressure, and grounded in actions and materials (not just words)

The initial activity leads to *planning*. Group members usually discuss what they have just experienced (individually and collectively) and then decide how they want to proceed. The planning includes a discussion of how both individual and group goals might be accomplished. Often students will make lists by brainstorming, identify the steps in a process, make models or diagrams, do short trial-runs, or break into small working groups and then reconvene to pool their conclusions. After that, each person decides what she or he wants to do for the next few sessions.

The next phase of the workshop, corresponding to the "middle" in traditional terms, includes the *actual workshop activities*. The instructor has the challenging task of assuring that materials and resources will be available to students while also being prepared to organize materials and resources *in response to their plans*. When students outnumber equipment, often some "traffic control" is required. For example, some ingenuity was needed to schedule use of the soldering tools when students were working with stained glass. Jim asked those waiting for the tools to teach one another particular skills and help their peers who were working on different steps of the process. Often a traffic jam can be avoided if students are encouraged to diversify their plans or to plan ahead and solve the tool-scheduling problems on their own.

In a guitar workshop, the instructor will need to find ways to keep the exploration interesting to beginners, who may lack the skills to do what they would like to do with guitars. He or she might choose to introduce the concept of chords, inviting a group of beginners to experiment with different sound combinations to create their own chords. These students might chart the new chords and then practice them together. Often the practice sessions spill over into informal time and self-scheduled time, as students who are focused on accomplishing goals (such as writing their own music) push to gain the specific basic skills they need.

Each workshop follows an individualized pattern, depending on the topic and on what the group has decided in their initial planning session. In some workshops, each meeting starts with an activity. In others, students begin each meeting by checking in and identifying ongoing tasks; then they proceed with their plans. In yet others, there are several phases to the work, each requiring that the group plan, learn new skills, teach skills to one another, and report their accomplishments to other subgroups.

In the final stage of a workshop, students work to finish what they have started, to *achieve closure*. In the Las Fallas workshop, the manual labor involved in making the figures turned out to be time-consuming. As the end of the week neared, students feared they would not have time to get the figures completed, dried, and painted. In a short meeting to talk over the situation, they decided to invite other students to help them with the papier-mâché during informal and self-scheduled time. This worked well. Not only did they finish their figures in time, but they also captured the interest and support of the entire community. Everyone then felt great investment in the concluding ritual burning ceremony.

In some cases, a workshop's final phase requires finishing products and deciding how to present or display them for the entire community. In other cases, such as the guitar workshop, the final phase involves a production, such as performing for a musicale or taping the music to be used in a video. In some workshops, students write up their discoveries (and workshop process) as an article for the Institute newspaper.

Help Students to Identify Tangible Products and Goals

It may seem unusual to focus on tangible products and goals in a program that is oriented toward exploring and gaining exposure to new things. Even in exploratory activities, however, it is important for students to achieve a sense of closure and a sense of achievement. Students have greater self-confidence when they see themselves as people who can get things done, make aesthetically pleasing objects, and solve problems involved in completing a task.

Too often in their lives, students sense that their achievements don't matter to anyone but themselves: Passing a quiz or completing a problem in an exercise book may not seem as significant to them as putting together a small performance that moves their peers or creating a model that can be displayed and discussed by others.

At the Institute, staff members grapple with the question of how to help students achieve excellence and at the same time allow them to participate on their individual levels while feeling unpressured and unjudged. What this means is that excellence must arise from the students' own passions and interests and definitions of success. The staff's role is to help students consider the aesthetic and practical issues that arise as they work on their various projects.

Repeatedly at the Institute both staff and student expectations are fulfilled and exceeded. The students build beautiful structures, put together impressive dramas and musical performances, create exciting and evocative skits, and know they are doing exciting, interesting work.

Use an Open-ended Questioning Style

Even with enticing materials and plentiful choices, students do not automatically leap into active, student-initiated learning. They may be too accustomed to waiting for teachers to tell them what to do. To gently redirect their attention to their own thoughts and interests, High/Scope instructors use an open-ended (divergent) questioning style.

As Corey mentioned in his discussion of Las Fallas, an open-ended question has no single right answer. Examples are "How do you feel when you look at this picture?" "How many different materials could we use?" "What might you depict in a Falla satirizing life at the Institute?" If a staff member offers students a direction for their thinking and then *stands back and allows discussions to develop*, student participation will usually, after some hesitation, gather momentum. The discussion will eventually bring out students' personal interests and thoughts.

Asking open-ended questions demonstrates to students that they have the ability to think things through themselves. This helps them to take ownership of their own learning process.

Open-ended questioning becomes a tool to direct students' attention to their own ability to think things through. When a student asks, "How do I do this?" the response might be "What are some ways you can imagine it being done?" If the student is truly stumped, the question can still be answered in an open-ended way: "Is there some way you can use wood or cardboard to make joints?" Other students can be called on to help: "Why not ask Tanisha if she has any ideas?"

By encouraging students to brainstorm, to list and then consider their options, the staff member gradually demonstrates to students that they do have the ability to think things through, to call on other students for help, and to learn through trial and error. This awareness helps students take ownership of their own learning process.

Open-ended questioning also encourages students to take more risks in their thinking. Willingness to take risks means exploring options, trying ideas on for size, experimenting, and using imagination and instinct as well as logic. When students are expected to give the "right answer," many stop thinking for themselves and instead spend their efforts trying to read the teacher's mind or live up to someone else's expectations.

Over time, students at the Institute begin to joke that High/Scope instructors always answer questions *with* questions. However, they also begin to see that they too have the ability to pose questions, to elicit opinions, and to give opinions freely. In that process, they discover the excitement of stumbling on interesting ideas and thinking of creative solutions to problems.

Engage Students Actively in Each Stage of the Process

Too often in group work there are only one or two active participants and the rest become passive observers. The High/Scope educational approach asks staff members to focus attention on making sure this does not happen with groups at the Institute. Because they are not busy lecturing or keeping order among unruly students, staff members have the time and energy to attend to students' individual needs.

Students have varying interests, abilities, attention spans, and levels of distractibility. When three students are happily engaged in cutting and affixing the wire mesh to a falla, for example, two others may well need help in figuring out what to do next or how to maintain interest. A staff member quickly learns who needs some help to remain engaged in an activity and who will respond to a simple reminder: "What's next on your plan?"

The timing, or pacing, of an activity has a great impact on students' successful participation. If one student is working with the welding torch while four others must stand around waiting for it, the waiting students will probably lose patience and become disinterested in the activity. Thus the staff member needs to think about how tasks can be spread out over time, what each individual can contribute, and what resources are available. The instructor's strategy of asking students to teach one another guitar skills worked well to keep everyone engaged in the guitar workshop.

When one student became bored with papier-mâché in the Las Fallas workshop, he began to act up, building towers of wood and steel rods he found sitting nearby and daring people to knock them down. Instead of shouting at the student for misbehaving, Corey asked him if he had considered the painting stage of the falla. Then he suggested that the student bring some paints to the place where the others were working and do some preliminary sketches.

Later when other students started to lose steam, he asked them how they might, as a group, make the activity more interesting. They decided to sing songs and make up verses while they worked. This made the experience enjoyable again, and the lagging members regained energy.

When an individual begins to lose interest in an activity, the staff member may decide to teach that student a new skill, asking him or her to then teach it to someone else. Other techniques are asking the student to take photos, to use a video camera, to select a new tool to work with, to shift perspectives

Staff take a supportive role, helping each student to contribute in a way that is personally meaningful.

or roles, to look again at the original plan, or to rethink the process. In some cases, the student may just need encouragement in seeing a difficult task through or a reminder of what his or her goals are.

If students see a way to participate and if the materials are available, they are generally anxious to be active. The staff member's task is to mentor—to help each student find a way to contribute that is personally meaningful. The group as a whole or individual students can also act as peer mentors in this regard.

Engineer for Success

All learning activities at High/Scope offer a balance between group collaboration and individual goal-setting. When students are choosing their own tasks, setting their own goals, working in a group context, and not being graded on the results, then success can be defined in new terms.

At the most basic level, staff attempt to create situations in which all students at all levels of expertise can be successful. This means being prepared with appropriate materials, making sure most of the problems that will be encountered can be solved, and making sure the necessary equipment and know-how are available to students when they embark on activities.

Staff also rethink their own definitions of success and encourage students as well to define it in unique and personal ways. One person's success might be a feeling of personal satisfaction or accomplishment. Another person's success might be recognition received from peers or staff.

Success can be audience response to a performance, or simply personal enjoyment. Success can be learning to make mistakes, to try something over and over until you get it the way you want it. Success for some students is learning to take risks, feeling the glow of friendship for peers that they might not have gotten to know back home, understanding how to solve a problem that has been causing difficult behaviors, and seeing their contributions matter to the people around them.

Contrast these definitions of success with the feelings many students have when writing a paper for a class. They know they are probably not saying something new, something that the teacher has not heard before. They realize that the teacher will be the only one to read what their efforts produce. They know that they will be graded on their thoughts and that in many cases, the grade will be best if they produce the thoughts the teacher seems to expect.

Many participants at the Institute have had little previous experience with success, personal or academic. At the Institute, the definition of success broadens and becomes inclusive of everyone. Staff members are trained to engineer for success by planning and facilitating in ways that allow each individual to contribute to the whole. When an activity is designed to be multilevel, each student is likely to find a level of success within it.

The Institute purposefully engineers for success in a number of areas where very few of the participants have had any previous exposure. For example, the folk dance workshop offered at all Institute sessions is taught using a progression of steps that builds basic skills, so the whole group experiences success and is willing and eager for more. With initial confidence built, the group is ready to move on to complex dances.

Throughout the month, the staff continually evaluates the "probability of success" of planned activities and instruction. Successive challenges are structured so each person can find a role and feel success in participating. Where needed, individuals are given help, most often by a fellow participant who has mastered a particular skill or process, so each person continues to feel included in the group's efforts and outcomes.

Encourage Students to Teach and Learn From One Another

Teachers and students too often assume that the teacher is the most knowledgeable, skilled, and therefore important person in the classroom. High/Scope's educational approach, in contrast, asks staff to structure their workshops so students come to see themselves and one another as resources. Jim met this challenge well in his workshop on stained glass. Although it was true that he had previous experience with stained glass and possessed the ability and knowledge to work skillfully with the tools, he set the activity up in such a way that students were increasingly able to turn to one another for guidance and ideas.

Peer teaching is possible in a setting where there is no single right answer to questions and where tasks have been broken down into manageable stages. Peer teaching is also more likely when a process of trial and error is built into the expectations. When students are engaged in projects each in their own way, they see natural opportunities to collaborate and share skills. However, when students are studying in "parallel" learning situations—when all are expected to learn the same things and master the same skills—competition creeps in, making collaboration less likely or spontaneous.

PROBLEM-SOLVING SKILLS AND PROCESSES

IMPROVISING

- Given a basic tune, how can you make it into a performance piece?

- Given a single measuring instrument, how can you use it to create others?

EXPLORING POSSIBILITIES

- Let's see how each shop tool can be used.

- What can be done with an oscillator?

- How many ways can you act out the concept *slow?*

BUILDING A BASIC COMPETENCY

- We will practice various ways to cut glass and then teach one another what we discover.

- What notes sound good together on the guitar? We are going to "invent" some chords, chart them, and create a song using them.

LEARNING A SPECIFIC TECHNIQUE

- We will explore the uses of an acetylene torch, with safety instructions, and use it to weld pieces of metal together.

- We will learn a folk dance and practice it, then choreograph our own folk dance, using the steps in new combinations.

CORRELATING OR MANIPULATING INFORMATION

- Everyone has been given a line from a poem. For the next few minutes we will circulate, reading our lines to one another and trying to identify the sequence the lines

Create Learning Opportunities Within the Context of Active Exploration

The Institute does not offer specific courses in math, science, or language arts, but staff do look for opportunities to explore mathematical concepts, scientific processes, and verbal and artistic expression within the context of ongoing activities. Students might learn how to use mathematics in figuring out the load-bearing capacity of various-sized balsa wood bridges. They might learn to write evocative imagery while trying to produce lyrics for a musical. They might learn about various chemical processes in analyzing the textures and functions of leaves.

Staff members think about the learning opportunities inherent in the design of their workshops or projects. What can be introduced, should follow. We will then assemble the lines in the order we think sounds right and create a performance piece from them.

- Given the concept of a "comfort zone" that exists around each person, we will experiment with how large our individual comfort zones are. Then we will gather some statistics to see if we can find any correlations between a person's comfort zone and his or her gender, race, age, interests, religion, country of origin, and favorite color.

DERIVING OR DETERMINING A PRINCIPLE

- For the evening program we will break into small groups. One group will try to figure out how much water is in the pond; another will try to calculate the number of blades of grass

in the side lawn; and a third will count the pebbles in the driveway. At the end, we will compare the techniques used to make the three estimates.

- The drama workshop is going to perform a series of silent skits, and we are asked to interpret what aphorism they are trying to communicate.

OPERATIONALIZING A CONCEPT

- We will explore the uses of negative space in making artistic sculptures.

- How can we use the force of gravity to move the canoes off their stands?

pointed out, or emphasized with students? In the Las Fallas workshop, Corey worked on the concepts of irony, satire, and ratio and proportion, among others. Jim worked on geometric angles, the physics of heat and light, and the chemistry of oxidation in the stained glass workshop. In an evening program, the whole group applied probability theory in exploring the concept of disease transmission. Students are continually exposed to problem-solving skills and processes in diverse contexts, so applying this kind of thinking becomes familiar to them. The insert above gives some examples of problem-solving skills and processes that students might experience and the contexts in which they might encounter them.

The more experience students have in a variety of realms, the more willing they will be to learn and to have confidence in themselves as learners. As students themselves try a variety of activities, *and as they watch their peers trying various options,* they develop a breadth that exceeds their own personal experience. They feel rewarded and enriched by the accomplishments of the entire community.

Endnotes

[1] The author, Corey Shouse, was a staff member at the Institute from 1990 to 1994. This account refers to the May 1992 Institute for IDEAS.

[2] Jim Brumberg was a staff member from 1987 to 1993.

5

Learning Potential Within the Institute Setting

In an integrated learning setting like the one that is created at the High/Scope Institute for IDEAS, staff members develop a different way of thinking about teaching. Instead of focusing on subject matter or didactic presentations to students, they learn to focus on *process*, on facilitating activities so they become rich learning opportunities.

High/Scope training helps staff to develop this focus by emphasizing the educational potential inherent in every aspect of the Institute program. During their training week, staff members spend time brainstorming about what teenagers can learn from the various elements of their day: What is the potential of group meals? What can be learned and experienced through a building project? What might arise as students share their individual skills and ideas with peers?

This discussion then progresses throughout the month, as staff are encouraged to look for educational potential in the workshops and other program offerings they plan, in the conflicts that arise between students, and in the room group relationships that are evolving.

Although Institute students do not all learn the same subject matter or all learn in the same ways, there are certain crosscutting educational elements of the program that everyone experiences. Students at the Institute

- Learn to participate in **groups** and to develop individual leadership abilities.

- Experience **work** as a task that engages physical, mental, and creative capacities.

- Develop an awareness of community and of how their actions can serve the wider community. This is the key to **service-learning**—which today is considered an important part of programming for adolescents.

- Exercise **higher-order thinking**—the capacity to use information and a variety of mental processes in the context of problem solving; they also begin to see the fruits of such thinking in concrete outcomes and achievements.

- Have significant interactions with accessible role models in an experiential context. They also experience and witness activities in a variety of fields and disciplines. This provides the basis for greater **vocational awareness** and aspirations.

- Experience a wide variety of ways to use leisure time constructively, gaining a basis for **consciously living** in a positive way and pursuing **healthful recreation.**

- Gain experience in creating a **shared culture** through the use of folk dance, singing, and consistent attention to the evolution of shared experiences. Because the setting provides effective ways to interact interculturally, interracially, and in mixed-gender groups, it enables students to experience open-mindedness and acceptance, sometimes for the first time in their lives.

Though some Institute students may return home talking enthusiastically about such specific activities as learning sign language, rewiring a lighting system, or going on a canoe trip, the crosscutting elements just listed constitute the true learning that the High/Scope Institute offers students. The remainder of this chapter elaborates on these elements.

Group Process and Leadership Development

By the third week of the Institute, we often hear participants complaining good-naturedly: "We aren't breaking into groups *again*, are we?" It is true that participants spend virtually all their time at the Institute in groups—working out the requirements of group living; planning activities together in room groups; eating and working together; collaborating on projects and learning tasks; and singing, dancing, and exploring together at evening programs. The Institute is structured in this way to create a cooperative community while fostering each student's awareness of what it means to be both a *member* and a *leader* within a meaningful context.

In a 1982 paper entitled "Group Process and Adolescent Leadership Development," High/Scope staff members Mary Hohmann, Douglas Hawker, and Charles Hohmann called this High/Scope's *leader-member approach to leadership development.* Underlying this approach is the belief that to be effective leaders and group members, young people must have opportunities to develop the interpersonal skills critical to both roles. Traits such as sensitivity to the needs of others, ability to accept and make use of others' ideas and contributions, tolerance for personal and cultural differences, and confidence in one's own skills and knowledge develop most effectively if students have multiple occasions to use these traits.

Institute staff members apply the following eight group strategies that help build the cooperative community and teach students to be effective leaders and group members. (This discussion is an adaptation, with permission, of the Hohmann, Hawker, and Hohmann paper just mentioned.)

1. Every Group Is Active

Each person is involved in planning, trying out ideas, solving problems, and putting things and ideas together. Staff members make sure that each individual can find a way to participate and that materials and challenges are plentiful. Even within situations in which some students are performing and others are the audience, the staff strives to make the observers aware of their role in supporting and responding to the performers.

In the course of each activity, staff members encourage students to work in pairs or triads, to mentor one another, to teach skills to one another, to share progress and results, to interact constructively,

Staff members encourage students to work in pairs or triads, to mentor one another, to share progress and results, to interact constructively, and to develop healthy conversational patterns in relation to their activities.

and to develop healthy conversational patterns in relation to their activities. In the final stages of an activity, the groups work together to plan presentations, to represent their accomplishments artistically, and to recognize the group process that has led to their achievements. Because each group is both active and interactive, students repeatedly have a concrete basis for knowing one another, which leads to deeper connections and a greater sense of respect for themselves and others.

2. Every Group Has a Purpose

The fact that groups form around goals tends to break down some of the hierarchical divisions that teenagers can often set up among themselves. Groups focusing on the arts or sciences work to produce performances, readings, presentations, demonstrations, displays, and tours. Groups engaged in work projects produce physical improvements—a safer stairway, a wider bridge, a prettier hillside, an additional hay wagon.

Group members define the desired outcomes of their efforts, and these outcomes ultimately are shared with the Institute community. This strengthens students' motivation, because each person has input and a personal stake in what the group is undertaking, and everyone is aware that in the end, the group presents its results to an appreciative and interested audience.

As various student groups form over the course of a month,

participants strengthen their abilities to invent, to solve problems, to understand, and to grow. Students' accomplishments have a synergistic effect on the growing self-confidence of their peers.

3. Every Group Is Cooperative

The lack of competition and the shared nature of tasks are two major factors in the willingness of small groups to make their outcomes public. Support, collaboration, encouragement, and success are far more effective motivators than competition is.

Because they find that in the Institute setting, others do not laugh at them, taunt them, cut them down, or judge them, community members of all ages are willing to try new things, to test hypotheses, and to share ideas and outcomes. *It is especially important for students to know that they will not be judged against their peers.*

Students learning in a collaborative context find that they can feel good about themselves not because their group accomplishment was better than someone else's but because they and everyone else enjoyed the vigor, the give-and-take, the excellence, the inventiveness, the performance, and the process they have experienced together.

4. Distractions Are Removed

For groups to form around meaningful goals, it is necessary to remove some of the trappings of teenage culture—the blaring boom boxes, the cigarettes, the pressures to act "cool" and to develop dating relationships. Adolescents no doubt take on many of the more negative teen trappings to give themselves an identity in the face of being ignored by the adult world. Were society to include adolescents as vital participants in communal endeavors, teenage culture would very likely look quite different.

In addition to asking participants to leave things like radios and junk foods at home, the Institute also helps them to reflect on the ways their usual habits differ from the mores that are quickly established at the Institute. As they see that they can have different types of conversations with one another and that they can accomplish many things, they often leave the Institute inspired with new ideas about how to spend time and use their energies. Being in a coed

environment that discourages exclusive relationships and cliques
enables students to see beyond the obligatory alliances of their often
restrictive social hierarchies to find new ways to create bonds with
fellow students.

5. Activities Are Designed to Forge a Community

A sense of community does not just happen when 50 teenagers come
together for a month; it is created through *communal activities*. It is
also fostered through the creation of shared history and shared
Institute culture.

At the Institute, as mentioned earlier, both folk dance and
communal singing offer shared experiences that become common
ground for community members. In addition, shared evening programs, field trips, communal meals, community meetings, and other
elements of the program provide consistent opportunities to come
together. Thus the community continually grows as an entity in each
individual's mind.

Evening programs regularly create community by promoting
group problem-solving, idea sharing, mutual laughter and fun, and
everyone's active participation. A good example of this was an
evening program in which students broke into groups of four; each
group was charged with the task of building a boat that would carry
a lit candle across the pond, enabling it to stay lit for the entire voy-
age. After each group designed and assembled its boat, the entire
community met on the beach, where each group in turn explained its
nautical theory. Then the flotilla set sail. Some boats burned, some
sank, and some made it across the pond, but whatever the fate of the
various boats, the esprit de corps was high, and the "Yacht Club"
became an important part of the community's shared history.

Work projects also call on the whole community from time to
time: asking everyone to gather in the garden, with various groups
each adopting a row of corn to weed; enlisting everyone in moving a
bridge from the wood shop down to its permanent place over the
stream; asking everyone to "turn" the volleyball court to make it
even and of regulation size. In all of these community activities, each
person feels the power of the total group and can see the importance
of his or her part in it.

6. Groups Are Engineered for Wide-ranging Experiences

When left to their own devices, adolescents tend to form groups according to the pressures of their social hierarchy. They like to hang out in cliques, often passively or actively rejecting students from other cliques. This exclusiveness may be a pattern that most of them have learned from their parents or from other adults in their communities.

At the Institute, staff members carefully structure, or "engineer," certain groupings to provide students with a wide range of interactions. The student-body at the Institute includes equal numbers of girls and boys; a fairly even distribution of ages; and a good mix of racial, ethnic, and cultural groups. From morning to night, staff see that these students are grouped and regrouped in diverse ways—into same-gender room groups; mixed-gender and mixed-age table groups; long-term groups or one-time groups; pairs or triads; and groups randomly selected from the whole community. In these diverse groups, participants encounter a variety of viewpoints and ways of doing things. This experience helps to break down their prejudices and preconceptions and enables them to practice tolerance and work actively to resolve the conflicts and compromises brought about by differences in human behavior.

Each Institute participant has the chance to eat, work, and learn with every other participant during the month. Living and working in small groups and eating at a table with eight other people calls for social skills many teenagers have had little chance to exercise— accepting another's point of view, listening, negotiating, sharing work and resources, carrying on inclusive conversations. These skills do not, of course, develop automatically; they are emphasized and modified by staff, supported by the diverse group structures, and called forth by the requirements of the Institute setting.

7. Voluntary Groupings Provide Choice

One element that makes groups work at the Institute is the fact that many groupings are voluntary. Participants choose their own daily instructional, work, or recreational groups based on personal interest and motivation. The only requirement is that each participant must choose *some* activity; the choice not to join, to do nothing, is generally not acceptable. But since real, exciting, and diverse choices are offered at each juncture, students rarely seem interested in nonparticipation.

In groups that are structured by staff (room groups, table groups, and most evening program subgroups), students are given wide latitude in the roles they will take on and their individual tasks. They are supported by staff in working through conflicts, in seeing the value of getting to know other community members, and in finding common ground even in random groupings.

The element of choice opens the door for students to be willing to get to know their peers. They are not consumed by resentment at having to be somewhere they do not want to be or having to do tasks they do not wish to do. Because of this, they are more open to engaging in the group endeavor at hand.

8. Staff Are Trained in Fostering Good Group Dynamics

Staff are potent role models from the very first day of the Institute to the very last. They are thus key motivators in the formation of community.

Some of the traditional expectations associated with classroom structure are not necessary for forming the types of groups promoted at the Institute. For example, being able to expound and hold group attention for long periods of time (as a lecturer does) is not important. No individual is encouraged to dominate a group setting at the Institute. Instead, staff members model a more low-key, peer-focused form of interaction. They learn to bring the attention repeatedly back to the students and to help students turn to one another for ideas, guidance, and support. Whereas classroom teachers traditionally work independently and are expertly versed in a particular subject, staff members at the Institute need to be good generalists who know how to work interdependently and to draw on diverse resources in the evolution of group explorations and activities.

For groups to be successful at the Institute, staff members need to master the fine art of inspiring engagement while getting out of the way of students' learning processes. It is a difficult role to assume. Some staff members seem to know instinctively how to practice "inspirational leadership/noninterference"; others struggle at each moment to find ways to contribute without dominating, to initiate without leading, and to guide without steering.

Although training can definitely help to develop this particular style of teaching, staff members also need to be mature enough to relinquish a certain amount of control, self-aware enough to share their strengths without overpowering the students, and well-rounded enough to be flexible in their goals for students and in their responses to events.

Work That Engages Physical, Mental, and Creative Capacities

In this era of high technology, "work" may sound old-fashioned. At the High/Scope Institute, however, physical work offers young people one of the richest learning contexts possible. Many students arrive at the Institute having done little physical work at all, and particularly, no physical work that, carried out over a sustained period of time, leads to a satisfying product or sense of completion. They are unaware of their physical capacities; inexperienced in working with tools or materials; and unfamiliar with the problem-solving processes inherent in building, landscaping, farming, and other physical tasks. For some teenagers "work" is a dirty word, made barely palatable only by its linkage to wages. The work they have done around their homes is rarely framed as an enjoyable, collective task with satisfying results.

One goal at the Institute is to give young people some positive experiences with work. They learn how to use their bodies in conjunction with their minds, how to combine tools and physical processes with creativity. They see that work can be enjoyable in itself as well as satisfying in its results. Thus staff and directors come up with projects that call for both planning and design on the one hand and physical effort on the other. Some examples of work projects (including projects mentioned in Chapter 3) are designing and building a lifeguard chair, rewiring and refurbishing display cases, landscaping an entranceway, creating a maze in a hay field, rebuilding a hay wagon, gardening, removing an old fuel tank, building an outdoor stage.

Work is concrete; it is immediate. It generally has clearly discernible results. When students have been weeding in a garden, for example, they can look back and see the difference between the weeded and unweeded sections; when they have been building an outdoor stage, they can see the work-in-progress and can use the finished product. Because of its concrete nature, work provides an ideal way to *connect ideas to action.* When students suggest the possibility of using a block and tackle to hoist an I-beam, they can test this hypothesis by physically implementing their suggestion and experiencing all of its real-life complications.

The Institute program calls on students to engage in two types of work: (1) *work to help take care of themselves and the facility,* such as cleaning, doing dishes, and maintaining the grounds, and (2) *creative work projects that lead to some kind of enhancement of their environment.* The first type, maintenance work, is addressed during morning cleanup time—in work crews—and in relation to mealtime. The second type is addressed through work projects, which generally meet for 12 to 15 hours over the course of the month-long Institute session.

One goal of the Institute is to give young people positive experiences with work. They learn how to use their bodies in conjunction with their minds and how to combine tools and physical processes with creativity.

These two types of work are used for somewhat different educational purposes. In introducing maintenance tasks to students, staff members emphasize the idea that the environment students live in belongs to them during the time they are at the Institute. Cleaning, washing dishes, picking up trash, and weeding the garden are all ongoing needs that the community is collectively responsible for. The emphasis during these times is on *recognizing what needs doing*—a skill that does not come naturally to many participants, on *working as a group to devise a system for getting work done,* and on helping students to become adept at *motivating themselves* and *attending mentally to the task.*

These are basic processes that students will use again and again in their lifetimes—in maintaining their homes and living spaces; in working to better their neighborhoods or communities; in providing safe and clean environments for their families; and in seeing themselves as responsible, active members in work and recreational settings.

Work crew tasks are not glamorous in the eyes of most participants. There is nothing exciting about sweeping floors, setting tables, or picking up trash. But as they do these things, they learn techniques for making work more enjoyable. They experiment with working in pairs, singing while they work, setting minigoals for themselves, creating small contests to see who can accomplish something the most efficiently, and having interesting conversations. They also learn to build up efficient work skills. They learn the intrapersonal skills of maintaining an inner sense of purpose; of motivating oneself; of dealing with fatigue, repetitiveness, and getting dirty; and of pacing oneself. They learn the interpersonal skills of sharing responsibilities, communicating about tasks, helping and asking for help, maintaining group energy, and bolstering that energy when it lags.

Students from recent Institutes might not recognize work crews in the above description. Most students treat work crew time not as a marvelous, life-learning opportunity but as an interlude necessary for maintaining their environment. But years after their Institute experience, students have reported that the work aspect of the program had a great impact on them: They had never before really used their hands, gotten dirty at tasks, or done much thinking about how meals got served or rooms got cleaned in their home environment. Their exposure to ongoing work at the Institute made them conscious of the physical efforts required to maintain home or work environments.

The primary goal of work projects is to help young people see themselves as capable of *creating, making,* and *doing* concrete things. From an array of offerings, students each choose the project that appeals to them. They then make a commitment to stay with that project over the course of several meetings. The projects span a range of complexity that usually includes some rather sophisticated building projects that will require the use of power tools and mathematical calculations; some more aesthetic, multifaceted types of projects, such as landscaping; and some projects that emphasize teamwork and simple, somewhat repetitive actions, such as haying or repainting an outbuilding. Regardless of their skills and experience, students are allowed to choose any project, and they are encouraged to try something new and challenging.

Staff members plan and design work projects to include collaboration, planning, using new skills and materials, reflecting on progress and results, and producing tangible outcomes—the same elements that are present in workshops and clubs. Throughout the projects, staff play a dual role of modeling energetic, enthusiastic participation and facilitating a group process in accomplishing tasks. Often they must teach new skills and help students learn to use tools or materials safely. Work projects are guided in a way that encourages students to use technical knowledge, problem-solving abilities, cooperation, mental imaging, physical strength, and social motivation to accomplish their goals.

Work projects often have a strong appeal to teenagers. It is exciting to think about rerouting a stream, constructing a gazebo, or creating a jogging path. For most Institute participants, this is their first opportunity to participate in something with such clear results. They are usually apprehensive about having the needed know-how and skills but proud to be part of such ambitious undertakings.

The learning opportunities built into work projects are rich and diverse. In planning a project, students employ models, create diagrams, use measurements and mathematical formulas, brainstorm and share mental pictures, examine examples of similar projects, and figure out what skills and experiences exist within the group. They then break the process into stages or steps; working in pairs and small groups, students individually choose the tasks and roles that they feel most comfortable with.

While doing the actual work, students once again confront physical reality: How can you use tools effectively? How can you pace yourself? How do you deal with fatigue, boredom, blisters, lagging partners? They also encounter multiple problem-solving opportunities: How can we remove this boulder? How can we join these two supports for greater strength? What welds are needed to reinforce the substructure? What materials will last and work most effectively here? How can we bind these two pieces together so they will glue properly?

As the project takes shape, students encounter questions of quality and durability: How do we make this new structure fit into the landscape? How can we install the chair so it will not eventually sag? How can we finish off these angles so they will be attractive? And once the project has yielded visible results, students frequently recapitulate their experiences for others, describing the steps and thinking and effort that have gone into creating their product.

The self-confidence built up in the course of work projects is tremendous. With justifiable pride, students rush to show their accomplishments to visitors. The projects are impressive. Former Institute students have reported that work projects made them feel they could accomplish anything. Work projects also gave them new awareness of their physical surroundings. They grew to appreciate the individual efforts that went into creating the objects and structures in their physical world.

Teenagers, while becoming increasingly capable of formal operational thinking (in Piagetian terms), still revel in opportunities to work in the concrete realm. And, in fact, being able to connect their thinking, problem-solving, and hypothesizing abilities to actual actions and objects enables them to integrate their experiences into a larger understanding. Work projects provide a vehicle for integration of thought with action.

It is ironic that contemporary culture has gotten so far away from physical work that many people must keep their muscles in shape by going to a gym to work out with weight machines or run on treadmills. The Institute gives students experience with using their bodies and exercising their muscles in the context of purposeful activities. Thus, it not only helps them to integrate mind and body, but it also provides feelings of competence of being able to contribute to and participate in projects in their communities.

Service-Learning

In "A Rationale for Youth Community Service," Joan Schine (1990) described how involvement in community projects can affect young people and the adults who perceive them in negative ways:

> Educators, youth workers (including members of the juvenile justice system), and other observers of society express anxiety about the growing alienation of our young. Although the media focus on "at-risk" youth, (the dropout, runaway, drug user and/or seller, teen parent), many more youth are simply aimless or alienated. Both a cause and an effect of this alienation are the negative perceptions of today's adolescents so common among adults. But when young people become involved in service in their communities, the "we/they" stereotypes of both young and old are replaced by new perceptions and understanding.

The Youth Community Service Schine referred to is a growing phenomenon. Increasingly, educators and youth workers are exploring the possibilities of reintegrating young people into the larger community through projects with older people, through volunteer efforts to help the homeless, through involvement in local school boards or city governments, through work in preschools or infant care centers, and in similar activities. Referred to as *service-learning*, these efforts can serve both young people and their communities.

In the same journal article, Joan Schine, citing Dorman, Lipsitz, Lounsbury, and Toepfer, stresses the benefits of community service for youth:

> Involvement in community service can meet many of the special needs of the early adolescent. . . . These include the need to:
>
> - develop a sense of competence, testing and discovering new skills;
> - discover a place for themselves in the world, to create a vision of a personal future;

- participate in projects with tangible or visible outcomes;

- know a variety of adults, representative of different backgrounds and occupations, including potential role models;

- have the freedom to take part in the world of adults, but also be free to retreat to a world of their peers;

- test a developing value system in authentic situations;

- speak and be heard, to know that they can make a difference;

- achieve recognition for their accomplishments;

- have opportunities to make real decisions, within appropriate limits;

- receive support and guidance from adults who appreciate their problems and their promise. (p. 7)

These needs are all addressed directly and indirectly through the High/Scope Institute for IDEAS programs. One of the primary goals is to *help students establish a sound base for ongoing involvement in their home communities.* We believe that for students to be successful in volunteer efforts and in community service projects back home, they must have support in developing a sense of community; they must have opportunities to work effectively with others and to see the value of their contributions.

Early on in the evolution of the Institute, participants would initiate ongoing discussions of how they were going to manage to "take camp home with them." "How can we keep being real?" they would ask. "How can we make our schools more fun and interesting, like this is?" "How can we ever explain what goes on here—it's so special?"

Staff members discussed this topic annually; community meetings, council meetings, and special evening programs would focus on identifying which specific elements made the Institute experience special and how students might create similar experiences back home. Some students were quite successful at doing so: One went home and started a guitar workshop with a group of her friends, encouraging their exploration and peer teaching. Another student started a speakers' program in her high school; it was run by a committee of students who brainstormed to come up with exciting topics and then canvassed their parents and community for volunteer speakers to cover the desired topics. They asked each speaker to use an activity as the basis of the presentation and to make the presentation participatory. Another student took a year off after high school graduation to volunteer in a multicultural preschool. One Institute alumna initiated "council" meetings with her basketball team.

School systems that sponsored some of the early program participants from diverse backgrounds (in Mississippi, Hawaii, and places abroad) reported that the students they sent to High/Scope (not necessarily their most outstanding students or school leaders) always returned changed. They rapidly became school leaders, initiated activities among their peers, improved their academic performance, and greatly contributed to the general well-being within their schools. This was true even of those who had been shy or underachieving before their High/Scope experience. (For sample quotes from some of these students, see "What School 'Just Doesn't Teach.' ")

This anecdotal proof of success led High/Scope program directors to look into specific ways to create a bridge between the experience at the Institute and the experiences students create for themselves or participate in within their home environments.

Educators in many school systems are particularly interested in how to get students engaged in meaningful activities in school and in the community. They see that eventually, many students who have shown high potential on tests or in their school careers drop out—emotionally, intellectually, and often physically as well. For example, two school systems in Michigan—the Detroit Public Schools and the Crawford, Ogemaw, Oscoda, and Roscommon (COOR) Intermediate School District in northern Lower Michigan—expressed interest in finding a way to use the Institute's approach with their disadvantaged students. They hoped to instill in them the willingness to achieve academically and to navigate successful paths in life.

WHAT SCHOOL "JUST DOESN'T TEACH"

"During talks at night with my room group, I learned so much about people from other races and it cleared up a lot of my misunderstandings. . . . I've learned not to judge things for what they look or seem like. Not only with people. There have been so many things here that when I first started, I thought I would hate, but they ended up being tons of fun."

• • •

"It [the Institute] changed me a lot. I used to not like to do work, and it helped me to quit smoking. It also helped me to learn stuff and meet new people."

• • •

"It [the Institute] caused me to think of teachers, from their point of view; it must not be fun for them either."

• • •

"High/Scope helped me realize that I won't get heard if I don't speak, and that I have a lot of good ideas and talent."

• • •

"It [the Institute] changed the way I think of people from other races. It proved my dad wrong."

• • •

"At school I've never fit in. But now I know I can be myself. I realize that everyone is unique, and that's okay. I can be myself and don't have to act up because my friends want me to. I'm getting along better in school and think that this year will be even better."

• • •

"If school were like this, I would think a lot more of school. I have learned things here that school just doesn't teach."

In response to these needs, High/Scope not only has developed the present Institute program as an experience for talented disadvantaged youth but also has addressed concerns about linkage by introducing the concept of *service-learning* to students; once students have experienced the Institute community and the gratification of seeing their contributions valued by others, they begin to ask how they can reproduce that experience back home.

Toward the latter part of the Institute session, staff members introduce the concept of service-learning. Students consider finding ways to be active, to address problems in their schools or home communities, to take a real role in community activities, and to establish ongoing interaction with interesting role models. Having experienced such things at the Institute, students find it a manageable and natural task to begin thinking about transferring Institute-like experiences to their home environments.

Students meet in small groups organized by geographical area (comprising all the students from the same school or same part of town) to discuss what concerns they have about their home community and how they might, individually or as a group, become active in addressing these concerns. A staff member meets with each group to help students translate their concerns into specific plans or strategies. This planning is very important to the success of the student-initiated projects. Since the students will be working independently once they are home, it is important that support be given at the Institute to help them develop the most thorough and feasible plans possible. Students develop plans that include such details as budgeting, scheduling, enlisting support in the community, and setting a date and time for taking the first step.

When students return home, they continue to meet with their service-learning groups, and a High/Scope staff member visits periodically to meet with the students and with interested school personnel and community members to help maintain project momentum. In these follow-up visits, emphasis is placed on helping students to identify resources in their communities. High/Scope's goal is to support students in forming the relationships within their communities that will allow their projects to be successful and long-lasting.

Sustained student interest and motivation are key to the success and duration of service-learning projects. Underlying sustained interest and motivation is student choice. When students choose to take on projects involving school or community problems that they are concerned with and that affect their lives, they are more invested than they would be in an assigned task or a volunteer task related to someone else's cause. In choosing a project to initiate and develop, students learn how they can be active citizens who influence the climate of their communities.

The Institute instills in young people a broad understanding of the many ways individuals can contribute to their community. The foundations for service-learning are built in a variety of ways throughout the Institute session: when a student becomes aware that his or her conversational style can "make or break" the atmosphere in a group setting; when a student stands before a group to teach a song or report on an activity; when several students see a problem through to a solution, then share their excitement with others; when young people participate in work projects or work crews; when someone puts aside his or her own task to take the time to teach skills to another person; when students have a successful community meeting or council meeting; and when students participate actively in the daily routine of the Institute community. Because the foundations for service-learning are clearly laid over the course of the month, students returning from the Institute ultimately find ways to make their home and school experiences more active, more communal, and more satisfying.

The distinction between service-learning and ordinary volunteerism is an important one to make when considering what sorts of activities service-learning projects will involve. For example, volunteering to do an assigned task (such as handing out flyers at a Red Cross blood drive) provides a valuable service. However, it does not promote personal growth and develop problem-solving skills in the same way that developing a voluntary project does. It is important for students to develop their *own* projects that address issues *they* have identified as problems in their community, and in which *they* are responsible for success or failure. Volunteerism that implies asking teenagers to sign up to take on preexisting roles in charity programs that they cannot truly influence can quickly cause students to lose interest in participating in community efforts.

Service-learning implies asking students—and adults—to devise voluntary activities that serve the larger community but serve their young participants as well: The activities should enable students to learn new skills; use their problem-solving abilities; and have opportunities to plan, initiate actions, and reflect on their contributions and experiences.

Students who have come through the Institute, though often profoundly affected and changed by their High/Scope experience, do not always become "super students" in the traditional academic sense. High/Scope produces ordinary young people who are *primed for success*. This priming does in many cases lead to greater academic and life success. It is most likely to do so when students find follow-up support available—from their school system, individual teachers, adult mentors, or parents.

High/Scope works (when possible) with representatives from students' schools and home communities to help create supports for students once they return from the Institute's enrichment experience. Academic settings are not always flexible enough to enable young people to find their place or feel seen and heard. State and national competency requirements often make greater student input and autonomy difficult goals to attain. However, even within these constraints, individual teachers, school systems, and communities are finding creative ways to support students in creating service-learning opportunities. (See "Two Service-Learning Projects" on pp. 174–175.)

Much work still needs to be done in this area, however, if all students are to receive effective support and guidance from the adults charged with their care and education. The principles that have emerged through experiences at the High/Scope Institute can be of use to all adults who are working to support young people in their development. Active learning, plan-do-review, collaboration, choice, service-learning, and the other concepts presented in this book can all be implemented in diverse settings, beyond the special and unique context of the High/Scope Institute for IDEAS.

Higher Order Thinking

Skeptics are wary of what they call the "fun and games" atmosphere of the active learning approach. They question how its seeming lack of system can ensure that youths are learning what they need to know to succeed in life. We have tried to show in this book that the open framework and the active learning approach at High/Scope are indeed systematic. However, it is a system organized not by subject matter but by the plan-do-review process. This process supports the development and application of thinking skills and creates in students a greater disposition toward flexible thinking. Research into higher order thinking supports this contention. In a 1993 article "Defining Higher Order Thinking," Lewis and Smith said this:

> *Higher order thinking occurs when a person takes new information and information stored in memory*

and interrelates and/or rearranges and extends this information to achieve a purpose or find possible answers in perplexing situations. A variety of purposes can be achieved through higher order thinking as defined above. These would include: deciding what to believe; deciding what to do; creating a new idea, a new object, or an artistic expression; making a prediction; and solving a nonroutine problem. (p. 136)

Based on evidence from 144 studies selected from a review of over 800 articles on the teaching of critical thinking, creative thinking, and higher order thinking, Underbakke, Borg, and Peterson (1993) identified five domains in their article "Researching and Developing the Knowledge Base for Teaching Higher Order Thinking." As they pointed out, "Teaching for higher order thinking is largely a matter of identifying and using . . . operations of thinking in the context of subject areas such as mathematics, science, language arts, and social sciences" (p. 139). They suggested that the kinds of thinking represented in the literature can be divided into these five domains:

1. *Hypothesizing and testing:* Conceiving connections among variables of a problem, and formulating and verifying these connections,

2. *Assessing arguments:* Identifying and solving problems that require evaluation of arguments,

3. *Solving interpersonal problems:* Analyzing issues and interpersonal problems and engaging in discussions leading to their satisfactory resolution, . . .

4. *Probabilistic thinking:* Resolving uncertainties when information is only partial . . . .

5. *Developing and maintaining flexibility and student awareness:* Keeping options open, evolving novel approaches to problem solution, and becoming aware of procedures and thought processes involved in solving problems. (p. 139)

In "An Example of Higher Order Thinking" (on p. 176), High/Scope students are called on to use abilities from each of

TWO SERVICE-LEARNING PROJECTS

Four former Institute students from Harrison, Michigan, decided that they wanted to repair and restore a run-down park in their home community. While at the Institute, they determined their goals, the main steps they would need to take, a time line, the people they would need to involve, the resources needed, a tentative budget, some fundraising strategies, and how they would initiate the project.

Back in their home community, over the course of several follow-up meetings with High/Scope staff members, the students made much progress. They first visited the park and listied all the repairs they wanted to make. Next, with a school counselor, they investigated the question of who owned the park. When they discovered that it was owned by the local township, they contacted the township board to ask for permission to work on the park and thus secured a place on the board's next meeting agenda.

They were subsequently invited by the board to present their plans and objectives and propose a budget. The board needed this information to make their decision and to determine if the township might be able to provide financial support. To prepare for this presentation, the students listed the park items they wanted to repair and the materials required.

Each student took responsibility for contacting some local businesses and individuals for prices and possible donations.

Their presentation to the board included a clear outline of their objectives, including blueprints of the structure they wanted to build. The township board was receptive to their ideas, and board members were impressed to see the students initiating a project for which they were not being given school credit.

Once their plan had been approved by both the township board and the park manager, they proceeded to approach local businesses to obtain the necessary supplies. By early spring they had secured paint and painting supplies, lumber and necessary hardware, basketball nets, diamond dust, and sand for a new sandbox. They had also begun to work closely with a teacher from their school, who became their primary mentor.

Work weekends were held in the spring and were carried out with the help of their mentoring teacher and a few friends they recruited from their school. The park is now much improved, and the students feel proud of their accomplishments. They were recognized for their accomplishment by High/Scope, their school administration, the township board, and their local newspaper.

High/Scope's major role in this project was to support students in their planning process and to work on encouraging local adult participation. Obtaining this local support made the project less dependent on High/Scope staff support, enabling it to continue beyond the follow-up initiatives.

● ● ●

Four students from Farwell, Michigan, wanted to address social issues in their community, such as abuse within families, alcohol and chemical dependency, and teenage pregnancies. They felt that their peers had inadequate awareness about these issues and no knowledge of where to go for information or help concerning them. The group's preliminary ideas about how to address this problem ranged from creating a local-resource guide to leading or arranging workshops in the schools.

Before planning the exact method for distributing information and raising awareness, research was needed. The four students first familiarized themselves with local services. They contacted local agencies to get information about the services available to their peers. During this process, they also inquired about what training might be available to prepare them to lead workshops or answer questions

directly. Having determined through their research that their efforts should be preventative in nature, the students decided to plan an Awareness Week for the middle school that would involve speakers from local agencies as well as interactive educational games.

The four students worked with their school counselor and social worker on logistics while they continued to meet periodically with a High/Scope staff member to work through planning and preparation of the event. With the help of the counselor, the group wrote a grant proposal and received $250 from the State Board of Education to use for their project. They involved their fellow students by holding a poster contest and by using student art to create a T-shirt, which they presented to the guest speakers in appreciation for their help.

The students' efforts resulted in three days of activities. Two guest speakers addressed the entire student body, and the service group participated by leading nutrition awareness activities and a disease transmission simulation. Planners and participants alike were pleased with the outcomes. In fact, the group has been encouraged by the middle school to plan another Awareness Week for next year.

AN EXAMPLE OF HIGHER ORDER THINKING

During one evening program, students are divided into small groups, where they are invited to design and construct a self-propelled vehicle. They may choose whatever materials they need from a large pile of raw materials in the center of the room. After 50 minutes, the small groups all assemble to demonstrate how their vehicles can propel themselves across the room. After each group's demonstration, students in the other groups are asked to describe why and how the demonstration vehicle worked (or didn't work).

Initially, group participants are invited to spend a short time exploring the available raw materials. They then break into their small groups to plan or design their vehicles on paper. In this stage of the process, students must decide what to do, call on any earlier experiences with or knowledge of vehicles, use their creative imagination to envision possi-

bilities, listen to one another and respond thoughtfully to each group member's ideas, grasp the essential ideas and extract the useable portions, communicate their ideas effectively, and delineate the steps of the process they will use.

The staff member helping them is there not to lecture but to support and coach them in thoughtful planning. Staff members ask open-ended questions and encourage students to evaluate each suggestion carefully. When a group is being somewhat conventional in its thinking, a staff member might ask, "Can anyone think of some wild or different way to modify this design?" Because it is not a teacher-centered activity, these kinds of questions are not heard as hints at right answers. Rather, they are considered as contributions by the staff member as a regular group-participant.

these domains. As they plan, they are proposing hypotheses and considering their workability by drawing models on paper. They use probabilistic thinking when they make estimations about the strength of various materials and the potential propelling power of various designs. As they discuss how they will go about the activity, they share creative ideas, developing flexibility and novel approaches to their problem solving.

As they gather materials and begin the task of construction, they must organize themselves as a group and resolve any interpersonal problems that come up, including domination or noncontribution by one or more members. As they look at how their peers' vehicles move, they must engage in hypothetical thinking, trying to analyze how the vehicles work, based on how they move and look. And in their group discussion of their perceptions, they must assess the arguments or thoughts of their peers and decide for themselves whether these explanations fit their own understandings.

The plan-do-review sequence, conducted in a cooperative learning context, repeatedly encourages applying abilities in the five domains identified in the "higher order thinking" schema of Underbakke, Borg, and Peterson. As students experience this sequence over and over in pursuing artistic endeavors, in conducting mathematical or scientific explorations, and in other group explorations and community problem-solving, it becomes a natural part of their learning cycle.

The Institute approach is congruent with the theories of Tishman, Jay, and Perkins (1993), who contended that it is not enough to have the ability to think a certain way; you have to be *disposed to use that ability.* An adult may well be *able* to consider other persons' points of view and may be able, for example, to describe someone else's perspective. But whether that adult regularly *uses* that ability determines the quality of her or his thought.

> Being a good thinker means having the right thinking dispositions. In this view, teaching thinking means more than inculcating particular thinking skills; it means teaching students to be disposed to think creatively and critically in appropriate contexts. . . . What characterizes a good thinker? To be sure, a good thinker possesses certain abilities: cognitive capabilities, as well as thinking strategies and skills. Yet what sets good thinkers apart is not simply superior cognitive ability or particular skills; rather, it is their abiding tendencies to explore, inquire, seek clarity, take intellectual risks, and think critically and imaginatively. These tendencies can be called "thinking dispositions." (pp. 147–148)

High/Scope's Institute program is designed to foster good thinking dispositions in a holistic environment that requires and

The plan-do-review sequence is a natural part of the learning process at the Institute. As students and staff discuss how they will go about an activity or experiment, they share creative ideas and develop new approaches to problem solving.

supports higher order thinking. This is why the program emphasizes high-quality role modeling by staff and asks teachers to encourage students to reflect continuously on their experiences, on their thinking processes, on the dynamics of their interactions, and on the efficacy of their plans or actions. Teaching subject matter, or even teaching thinking skills per se, is not emphasized, since these are best learned in the context of real tasks and personally meaningful processes.

Tishman, Jay, and Perkins (1993) support the High/Scope approach when they suggest that good thinking dispositions are best taught through the "Enculturation Model" of teaching—"a model that emphasizes the full educational surround" (p. 150). They identified (on p. 148) seven thinking dispositions and the tendencies they include:

1. *The disposition to be broad and adventurous:* the tendency to be open-minded, to explore alternative views; an alertness to narrow thinking; the ability to generate multiple options.

Example—In a mask-making workshop that culminated in a dramatic performance, one student decided that rather than use plaster and paints to create a mask that represented a face, as everyone else did, she would use a variety of natural materials from outdoors to create an abstract representation of her "inner self."

2. *The disposition toward sustained intellectual curiosity:* the tendency to wonder, probe, find problems; a zest for inquiry; an alertness for anomalies; the ability to observe closely and formulate questions.

Example—One day in the dining hall, a 15-year-old girl from Detroit stood up with an announcement: "At our table we are all wondering why we see our reflection upside-down when we look at the front of the spoon but right-side-up when we look at the back of the spoon. We'd like you all to discuss it among yourselves and give us your theories in 10 minutes."

3. *The disposition to clarify and seek understanding:* a desire to understand clearly, to seek connections and explanations; an alertness to unclarity and need for focus; an ability to build conceptualizations.

Example—In a work project that centered around the restoration of an old piano, one student expressed his confusion about the actual source of the sound heard when piano keys are played. He wanted to explore the physics of sound, and not just the physical connection between the hammer, the string, and the piano key. After the group explored the ideas, they decided that in conjunction with their restoration project, they would present to the rest of the Institute an explanation of sound waves and hearing.

4. *The disposition to be planful and strategic:* the drive to set goals, make and execute plans, envision outcomes; alertness to lack of direction; the ability to formulate goals and plans.

Example—A group of students sought the support of a staff member in planning an evening program called the International Festival. Their goal was to educate others about cultural traditions from various countries as well as to celebrate the diversity of back-grounds included in the Institute group. They formed a planning committee and saw that each person took on some task: decorating, locating supplies, finding representatives from various countries, researching foods, or developing short activities. When discussion of the event became unrealistic at times, one student continually reminded the group of its goals.

> 5. *The disposition to be intellectually careful:* the urge for precision, organization, thoroughness; an alertness to possible error or inaccuracy; the ability to process information precisely.

Example—In a work project that involved building a lifeguard chair, students began by building a balsa wood scale-model of the proposed chair. They used the model as a basis for discussing and hypothesizing about such important issues as the ergonomic correctness of the seat and the appropriate distance to sink the chair legs into the ground for stability.

> 6. *The disposition to seek and evaluate reasons:* the tendency to question the given, to demand justification; an alertness to the need for evidence; the ability to weigh and assess reasons.

Example—Following a recycling work project, a group of students approached the facility managers to ask why styrofoam cups were used on Sundays for outdoor cooking. When a reason was given, students initiated research of their own to verify the ecological safety of using styrofoam. The students came up with two alternatives: using a cheaper and safer plastic foam cup that could be thrown away or using recyclable styrofoam cups and saving them and taking them to the closest recycling center.

> 7. *The disposition to be metacognitive:* the tendency to be aware of and monitor the flow of one's own thinking; alertness to complex thinking situations; the ability to exercise control of mental processes and to be reflective.

Example—During an evening council, a student expressed concern about his tendency to "ostracize" some people at the Institute. He explained that he was used to feeling left out both at home, because of younger siblings, and at school, because he wasn't part of a large, popular group. He realized that he was making assumptions about others' attitudes toward him and then reacting to those assumptions in the way he treated them. He apologized to people whose feelings he may have hurt and said that he is trying to be more aware of his actions and how they affect others.

It would not be realistic to expect the High/Scope Institute to foster all seven of these dispositions in every student in the course of four short weeks. Nevertheless, as students experience and share the hundreds of ongoing activities at the Institute, each and every one of them is repeatedly asked to call upon these seven dispositions. They are constantly meeting situations that require planful, higher order thinking and reward its use with tangible results.

Vocational Awareness

An informal survey of the employees in most organizations and professions will show that a variety of paths have led people to their present positions. Some chose their job or profession at an early age and then trained with great purpose to achieve success in it. Others were steered gradually toward their vocation through school, family, or community influences, in response to life experiences. Many were inspired by a role model. Some professionals chose a career after completing college, trying a number of vocational possibilities and then going back for specialized academic training. And a surprising number ended up in their occupation through a series of happy coincidences or unexpected opportunities.

Despite widespread knowledge about this diversity of successful paths, there is a trend in education toward pressuring students to know clearly and early on what they want to be when they grow up. Many middle school and senior high school curricula call for increasing academic specialization, early decision-making on the part of students, and premature tracking of students according to future aspirations or present ability.

At the High/Scope Institute, the approach to career education is framed by these general principles: (1) providing *exposure to possibilities* by giving students concrete experiences on which to base future predilections or study; (2) providing *multiple role models* whom students can get to know in action; and (3) providing plentiful opportunities for *exploration, trial and error,* and *generalized skill building.* Vocational topics per se are introduced in a collaborative, interactive context (through a three-day college and career workshop and various field trips). Throughout all Institute activities, High/Scope's goals are to expand students' ideas about what is possible, to help them gain a stronger belief in their ability to do whatever they choose, and to inspire them to achieve. Each of the three general principles behind High/Scope's career education can be described in more detail:

Exposure to Possibilities

In a standard vocational or career-training program in the schools, students generally attend a half-day seminar or an hour-long counseling session in which they are exposed to vocational possibilities. They are typically given lists of possible careers and presentations on the careers by visiting speakers. While this is better than no exposure at all, it is like trying to buy shoes from a catalogue—there is no way to "try on" the chosen profession before buying it.

We believe that exposure to various vocational possibilities is most effective if it can include active participation. Students need to experience activities that typify a whole variety of occupations; they need to be given a chance to play with the skills, modes of thinking, and subject matter that are representative of those occupations. It is also useful to help students build up their general interest-level, motivation, skills, and pool of experience. They need to see how the skills and concepts they are learning can be applied in the real world. This is a reversal of the more traditional approach, in which possible vocations are presented and then students are told what they must study in order to enter them.

A different approach to career exposure is taken at the Institute. As students work on the community's newspaper, for example, they learn to use computers competently; they work on design elements and skills and consider formatting, printing, and production issues. They gain experience in creative writing, journalistic reporting, and summary writing; they learn to conduct opinion surveys and analyze trends. In this process, many possible careers are touched on: writer, poet, computer technician or programmer, designer, journalist, technical writer, musician, sociologist, publisher. The staff member working with the newspaper is conscious of each of these career links and may mention one or another of them casually in the course of events or may ask the students at some point to brainstorm about where and how they could later use the skills they are learning while working on the newspaper.

As another example, a project in which Institute students build a corncrib bridge includes elements of drafting and design; historical research (interviewing the corncrib donors about its history and preparing a plaque); transportation (moving the bridge safely back to camp); engineering and construction; landscape architecture; welding and other tool use; and investigation of weather patterns and water cycles (determining the river's high-water point).

A student dramatic production entails acting, of course, but it might also entail literary interpretation and critique; psychology (understanding characters and their motivations); ensemble work; improvisation; musical composition; electronics (creating a sound score); construction and art (creating scenery); sewing and costume design; and cultural interpretation (working to create meaning).

The evening program exploring disease transmission (the simulation game described on p. 72 [Ch. 3]) includes thought processes related to several areas of endeavor: epidemiology, sociology, behavioral science, medicine, chemistry, public health, business, and sex education.

For each Institute participant, these individual experiences multiply and take on depth over a month of active learning programming. Secondhand exposure to others' career-exploration experiences is also a factor as students regularly share their products and processes in the presentations that small groups make to the Institute as a whole. Late-night conversations in room groups are another powerful means of sharing. Together, these experiences present a matrix of possibilities that seems rich and varied indeed.

Multiple Role Models

Most teenagers have limited opportunities to know people older than themselves, from a variety of occupations. Disadvantaged young people, in particular, may encounter few professionals other than educators (teachers) and social workers. If they are lucky enough to be part of a church or community group, they may know people employed in a greater variety of jobs but never have the opportunity to learn about their occupations or see them at work.

Yet it is clear that role models are potent motivators for young people. Negative role models abound: peers who pressure for antisocial behaviors; adults who are forbidding rather than compassionate and understanding; parents who are unemployed; gang members who pressure young people to choose sides early; and jaded older youths who encourage young teens to hide emotion and to quash enthusiasm. Positive role models are often sports and movie stars whose wealth, beauty, and athletic ability are inspiring but do not necessarily provide realistic guidelines and expectations for young people trying to develop a sense of self. It is crucial to counterbalance these types of role models with equally compelling role models who present realistic, positive alternatives.

Institute staff members, as described earlier, are chosen for their diversity, their enthusiasm, their multiple interests, and their orientation as generalists. Though they may have majored in particular areas of study (not necessarily including teaching) they have also had various job and field experiences. Some may work in fields considered nontraditional for their gender—for example, a woman may be an engineer, or a man may be a nurse.

The most salient aspect of staff members' role modeling is the fact that they live and interact continuously with students throughout an entire month. The students have abundant opportunities to ask staff about their experiences, to listen to their insights and ideas, to connect life choices with life-style choices, to think about the questions of what is possible and what one needs to do to realize dreams.

Staff members are trained to be conscious of their role modeling—to build on the bonds they form with students, opening their minds to greater possibilities and helping them to identify the concrete steps they can pursue in achieving their goals.

Exploration, Trial and Error, and Generalized Skill Building

A career-development professional from a large state university complained to us that she once tried to bring together a group of students very similar to those at the Institute (disadvantaged rural and urban youth) for a two-day career workshop. She dubbed it the worst flop of her career. The students not only refused to interact with one another; they were entirely unresponsive to the adults who had been carefully chosen as "good role models." Instead of taking advantage of this special event cosponsored by their schools and the university, the students were passive and uncommunicative.

This failure does not seem surprising. Students who are accustomed to viewing themselves as failures and who come from unstimulating home environments need to be given time and real opportunities to get past the habits of passive noncooperation. The old saying that you can lead a horse to water but you can't make him drink is apropos. However, if you provide the horse with water *in a safe, appropriate environment,* then he is more likely to drink—when he gets thirsty.

The career-development professional did not have the luxury of controlling the context in which her students met. But educators, and many vocational professionals, do have some say about the context of vocational exposure. When learning is made enjoyable and when students are allowed to engage in "subvocational" activities—that is, activities leading to awareness of the processes, thinking, and tools of various vocations—they are more likely to be ready to engage in dialogue about their vocational futures. The key elements of subvocational activity are *exploration, trial and error,* and *general skill building.*

- *Exploration* allows students to expand their mental map of the universe: What is possible? What do various choices entail? What does it feel like to try out activities associated with various fields?

- *Trial and error* allows students to develop a willingness to explore, to try things out, to make mistakes and keep going, and to continue to believe in their potential even in the face of setbacks.

- *General skill building* helps students to feel competent. This in turn leads to greater self-confidence. Building general skills enables students to have a solid base from which to perform creatively and competently in their lives. They see that they can learn new skills; they discover their personal learning style; and they learn to use their general skills as a basis for acquiring specialized skills later on.

After a month at the Institute, most students go home with an array of new skills. Although having these new skills might not immediately lead to a job or suggest a clear career path, it greatly affects students' attitudes and future efforts. Girls who have learned to use tools are more willing to consider nontraditional careers; students who have become familiar with computers are more likely to seek out further training or experience with them. In general, more kinds of activities seem possible, comfortable, and appropriate to students after their month of active engagement at the Institute. (See "Changed Attitudes.")

Conscious Living and Healthful Recreation

> Responsible citizenship in our society requires not only a broad fund of knowledge but also a range of social competencies that include such life skills as social problem solving, decision-making and skill in evaluating powerful media messages and persuasions. Our society is reevaluating the educational system. . . . However, there has been very little attention paid to preparing our youth for successful adult life in the areas that fall outside the boundaries of traditional formal school criteria. (Hamburg, cited in Pittman & Wright, 1991, p. 2)

With this quote from Beatrice Hamburg, Pittman and Wright make the point that preparation for adulthood goes beyond formal schooling. Young people's outside experiences can be significant exposure as well. Not every interest an adolescent is exposed to leads to a career. But having constructive interests outside of work can help people to become more informed, more satisfied, healthy citizens who are

CHANGED ATTITUDES

"The camp changed me. I want to study abroad. I want to learn a new language and another culture and meet even more people just to learn. I'm now more curious than ever."

"The university field trip was a good experience for all of us. It got me really thinking about college and different college majors."

• • •

"I probably can't make a huge difference to help the world or to solve the world's problems. But my time here helped me realize that I make my own attitude and I control my own actions. I can make the world around me here better. I can help the people I see, I can be nice to people, and I can be there for them. This is the world where I can make a difference for good and we all can. We've got to reach out to others. The Institute helped me realize that I want to be a nurse. That way I can help people through my career too."

able to participate in the fabric of their communities. At High/Scope we believe this avocational aspect of living is important. We train staff members to support students' development of living and recreation skills, which can help them lifelong in becoming engaged and satisfied family members and community members.

Too often, teenagers' time is divided between academic work, which many of them feel apathetic toward, and passive recreation —pursuits such as watching TV, playing video games, or "hanging out." Young people who lack adult supervision after school fall easily into nonproductive or even self-destructive habits. As a result they frequently not only fall behind academically but also fail to thrive in their social and emotional development.

Extracurricular activities, girls' and boys' clubs, and other youth organizations can provide young people with some of the social and emotional challenges necessary to becoming healthy, active adults. Often, however, such activities are only available in wealthy communities, or they conflict with a young person's need to earn money to help support the family, or they fail to attract the young people who could most benefit from their offerings (Pittman & Wright, 1991).

At the High/Scope Institute, students are exposed to the idea that learning and living are inextricably bound. Academic studies are useful to help prepare students for some of the tasks they will face in earning a living, but they are only part of what educators must attend to. Adolescents also need to learn how to function effectively and how to have their needs met in a personal and social context. For this part of their education, educators, parents, and other community members share responsibility.

We *all* need to ensure that young people do not fall between the cracks as they struggle for economic survival and internal equilibrium. When a program for teenagers *integrates* attention to living and avocational concerns as part of its culture (instead of tacking these on as extracurriculars), young people are likely to thrive on all fronts: personal, social, and academic. The following is a description of the attention paid to *conscious living* and *healthful recreation* throughout the Institute session. We intend not to make value judgments about which habits are better than others, but rather to give students a laboratory in which to examine the cause-and-effect relationship between life-style choices and quality of life.

Living Skills

One goal of the High/Scope Institute for IDEAS is to help students develop numerous living skills, especially ones related to health, group living, taking care of the environment, problem resolution, making friends, and work.

Health. The topic of health is not elective—it is crucial for everyone. Teenagers in particular need to learn to care for their bodies, to pace their energies, to choose nourishing foods and activities, and to come to terms with their sexual feelings, learning to behave responsibly and safely.

Because the Institute is a residential program, where we have excluded the use of drugs and stimulants and the common teenage distractions, it is a unique opportunity to lay the groundwork for students' long-term habits by modeling physically healthy and socially wholesome behaviors.

Students often initially complain when we ask them to leave junk food at home and do not provide it at the Institute, but this generally leads to valuative discussion as they begin to see how different they feel when they are eating nutritious meals, engaging in regular physical activity, and sleeping a reasonable number of hours each night. For some participants, this life-style is radically different from what they experience at home. In particular, students who suffer from bulimia, anorexia, and compulsive eating get support from staff in facing these behaviors, which are difficult to hide in a community with regular communal habits.

Often the students themselves address issues of hygiene. In a recent community meeting the topic was discussed at length before most students realized that some community members just did not own enough clothes to wear clean ones daily. This was a very sensitive issue, and the students displayed great tact as they explored possible solutions, such as asking the Institute to provide free soap and shampoo in all the bathrooms, encouraging everyone to hand-wash dirty shirts and underwear, and encouraging shower times for everyone on a regular basis.

Without the pressure, or opportunity, to be sexually active, young people are often free to explore other aspects of their sexual and gender identity. The many opportunities for discussion and self-expression often allow students to get a clearer sense of themselves and their feelings for others. We address social/sexual issues such as sexually transmitted disease, boy-girl relations, and social-sexual peer pressure throughout the program in a low-key manner that gives students a way to explore these topics without embarrassment. Many of these issues become topics for council reflections, subject matter for dramatic presentations or skits, and topics of nighttime room group conversations.

Staff members participate and model responsible attitudes in these health-related discussions and activities. They help students to consider all sides of a question and to examine the prejudices and expectations that they place upon one another and upon themselves.

Group living. Skills in group living, while not identical to family-living skills, can often transfer to family life and other situations. Staff members are conscious of helping participants learn to share meals harmoniously (or, at the very least, courteously). This includes learning to engage in constructive rather than destructive conversations and recognizing that both noise and silence have an impact on others. It also includes learning to assess how much food is available and to be conscious of sharing. It includes taking turns serving one another, setting and cleaning tables, and being aware of general table etiquette.

The Institute gives a bit more emphasis to room groups than many residential programs do, in an attempt to help young people become more aware of themselves and one another. As participants work out the sharing of physical space (sleeping areas, bathrooms, showers) and emotional space, they learn to reach compromises between their personal desires and those of the group.

Taking care of the environment. Care of the environment is often left to custodial staff in schools and to parents in homes. Yet, when paying attention to the facility and its maintenance are emphasized with young people, many of them begin to see that their surroundings do make a difference. They are able to make connections between their small, individual actions and the larger, global issues of environmental concern.

Many teenagers have never thought about the concept of setting a mood. At the Institute, this includes such things as maintaining a respectful silence while watching a performance or listening to others speak; landscaping, building, and decorating to create a pleasing visual atmosphere; and cleaning to create a comfortable and sanitary setting. Once they have experience with this concept at the Institute, students can begin to think creatively about how they can contribute to and shape the environments they participate in back home. Although many of them come from neighborhoods and homes that reflect poverty, danger, and disrepair, they see that with ingenuity and group cooperation, they can still make some changes to improve their setting for themselves and others.

Problem resolution. Many students come from homes with violent or dysfunctional relationships. Therefore, at the Institute, students are provided with daily, ongoing exposure to problem resolution, which gives them new ideas and new skills in behavior. They learn that they can talk through a conflict, reframe their understanding, articulate their disaffections, and constructively order their thoughts. They become skillful in proposing solutions, plans, and compromises.

We do not want to make this sound idyllic. With 50 young people from relatively difficult backgrounds, there are numerous conflicts or spats and even occasional threats of violence. But through the redirection of energies into constructive activities and through the daily efforts of staff, who walk students through different thought processes or ways of behaving, many of the students are able to transform their antisocial habits and develop greater flexibility, kindness, and consideration.

Making friends. Although making friends may not seem like a curricular topic, it is of concern to most people throughout their lives. At the Institute, students are able to get below the surface of their friendships with one another, getting to know people (outside their families) better than ever before.

They learn new definitions of intimacy: to live respectfully with people you are not related to, to trust someone to support you in the context of an activity, to express opinions on topics of great personal concern in front of peers from diverse backgrounds, to sing or talk or dance in front of a group.

Because students get to know one another in the context of activities and in an environment that promotes racial and gender respect, they learn that people cannot merely be labeled as friends or enemies. They learn to like someone whom they might ignore back home, to be friends with someone of the opposite sex in a nonromantic way, and to form alliances based on shared interests rather than on social status.

With staff support, many students are able to get past some of the self-hatred or self-defeating habits that are products of their past. The program gives them real reasons to like themselves and to feel successful, and they gain a clearer sense of their value and membership. With regular meals, a high level of activity and interest, and physical exercise, some students discover that their moodiness and depression are considerably lessened. The program does not remove their problems or the pressures they live with back home, but it does offer many of them an oasis in which they can heal their spirit.

Work. We have already addressed *work* to a large extent on page 161. Here, we want to stress that although young people are usually given little opportunity to develop the intra- and inter-personal skills related to work, these are skills that they will use throughout their lives. They benefit tremendously from the opportunity to experience their emotional and physical reactions to work tasks. As they learn how to motivate themselves to get started on a task, to sustain attention, and to find personal meaning in their activities, they develop intrapersonal skills that can transfer to home and occupational situations. Similarly, as they learn to collaborate effectively on work tasks, they get to develop interpersonal skills many academically trained professionals lack: ability to plan collectively, to share tasks, to communicate in order to make work flow more smoothly, and to cooperate in completing a complex project.

Healthful Recreation

> There is general concern about the decline in leisure reading and hobbies among adolescents and adults as television watching and video game-playing increase. There is also popular interest in "leisure education" as an emerging growth area (e.g., non-credit adult education) as people live longer after retirement and have more leisure time during their working years and growing academic interest in the role that leisure time use plays in adolescent development . . . (Pittman & Wright, 1991, p. 13).

This quote from Karen Pittman and Marlene Wright explains and supports High/Scope's emphasis on students' making good use of their "free time" at the Institute. We believe that in most programs for adolescents, the dichotomy between leisure time and academic time is too strict. It does not reflect the *integration* of experience that teenagers crave and need. Therefore, at the Institute staff try to present free time as a viable programming unit, to be used creatively and purposefully.

After a month at the Institute, students go home with many ideas about how to spend their free time. They also go home with a new understanding of their interests and of the potential of shared activity. The Institute not only expands their ideas about what types of recreation they might engage in but also suggests new ways to structure leisure activities and integrate learning with living. The recreational skills that students develop include the ability to structure time, to plan and organize events, to find and use materials, to participate in noncompetitive sports, to engage in constructive conversations, to promote inclusive activities, to practice collaboration and leadership, and to develop hobby (nonvocational) interests.

Structuring time. One of the strongest components of healthful recreation is knowing how to structure time. As students see what they can accomplish in the half hour after breakfast, or during a quiet reflective time, or in the self-scheduled time that is available each afternoon, they begin to realize that planning their time can enhance recreation.

After a month at the Institute, students go home with many new ideas about how to spend their free time and a new understanding of their interests and of the potential of shared activity.

The highly scheduled day at the Institute helps students to recognize that varying their activities can be a good way to keep up their interest and energy. Too often adults get in the habit of simply alternating between work or collapse. After a long day at the workplace, they fail to consider sports, artistic explorations, music, or other recreational activities as renewers of energy. They generally find themselves in front of the TV, wishing they had the energy to engage in projects.

Planning and organizing events. Knowing how to plan and organize their own events helps students to feel autonomous. Once they have seen that they can create interesting self-scheduled activities, teach one another skills, share what they have learned, put together a dramatic performance, organize a hike or canoe trip, and initiate a discussion or meeting, students are not likely to wait around passively to see what activities adults will provide for them. As they return home, many students carry on long discussions about activities they would like to organize among their friends or in their schools. They are not content to return to their former routine of "hanging out"; instead, they have specific ideas about how they might change their patterns of leisure activity.

Finding and using materials. Many disadvantaged students do not have the equipment or materials required for recreational pursuits. For this reason, Institute staff members emphasize ways to use recreational materials that are not costly and that are easy to scavenge. Students are encouraged to brainstorm with peers to figure out where they might get the materials and resources they need for the projects or activities they would like to undertake. They also discover that they can have the use of some equipment or materials through their schools or community groups if they only think to ask. At the Institute, young people learn that it is okay to ask and that adults can be supportive allies when it comes to accessing materials.

Sports time at the Institute often involves creative, cooperative games that are new to most students. However, traditional sports like soccer are also played, with new rules that de-emphasize competition.

Participating in noncompetitive sports. As mentioned before, High/Scope promotes inclusive, noncompetitive sports. Not only does this convey the values of sharing, teamwork, and peer support, it also allows participants to discover that recreational sports are good for the body, socially enjoyable, and open to everyone.

Many times minority youth, especially males, are pressured to take sports very seriously. Because their major role models are sports heroes, they see sports as an avenue to fame, success, and even higher education. While taking this path may work for a small number of young men, for others it is not a realistic choice, and their exclusive focus on sports does not allow them to develop other abilities.

For the true athletes among the students, it is not harmful to have the Institute experience of considering the less competitive, more collective, aspects of team effort. For the rest of the students, we feel that the Institute approach to sports is essential to helping them experience healthful recreation and fun. As in the case of Cynthia, who always avoided physical activity because she had been teased about her weight, it is crucial that young people have opportunities to learn to use their bodies in enjoyable, supportive contexts.

Engaging in constructive conversations. The Institute places continual emphasis on constructive conversation, which is an important dimension of recreation. An activity can be either enhanced or degraded by the kind of conversation participants engage in. If students sit around complaining about their lives and bad-mouthing their peers, they perpetuate a negative, nonrewarding ethos and also fail to take advantage of the potential for an exciting, engaging moment.

As people work or share meals or walk from one place to another, they talk. Throughout the day, there are multiple opportunities for communication, discussion, and idle chats. As students become aware of positive conversational strategies and tones, they are able to engage more deeply in their work, their social relationships, and their communications. They also feel better about themselves and their community.

For many young people, talking is a major pastime. Any parent of a teenager who has waited for hours to gain access to the family phone will attest to this. Therefore, it is useful for students to consider what styles of conversation they engage in and what impact their verbal participation (or nonparticipation) has on their peers and family.

Promoting inclusive activity. The Institute policy of promoting inclusive activity means that all activities are open to all participants,

As students become aware of positive conversational strategies and tones, they are able to engage more deeply in their work, social relationships, and communities.

and we encourage participation based on voluntary choice in most situations. When students see that this enables them to learn from and get to know a broad variety of people in a multitude of ways, they often abandon their ideas of exclusivity. Since inclusion is one of the key factors in developing open-mindedness, it is an important dimension of both leisure and formal activities at the Institute. The attitude of inclusiveness that people learn at the Institute exposes both students and staff to new ways of doing things, to new approaches and energies. It also helps to discourage the formation of in-groups and out-groups, which is common among teenagers (and among some adults as well).

Practicing collaboration and leadership. Collaboration and leadership are addressed at length in other chapters of this book. Both of these play a role in all the recreational and leisure activities at the Institute, teaching students to think in terms of constructive group endeavors.

Developing hobby interests. The decline in hobby interests among young people and adults (mentioned earlier in the quote from Pittman and Wright) is due in part to television and video games. But among disadvantaged youth, it is also due to lack of exposure and lack of adult leadership in learning about possibilities. After a month of broad active experiences with art, music, drama, dance, construction, computers, nature, science, math, writing, folk dance, sports, and social explorations, students go home with specific ideas about what interests they might want to develop further.

Schools too often teach only to the future experts and professionals. Many high school English classes, for example, tend to prepare students to be English majors in college and English professors after further graduate study. But there is also a large segment of students who can profit from courses in reading appreciation as opposed to literary criticism. Similarly, there are students who might like to take courses in science appreciation, math appreciation, art appreciation, and other similar topics. Community colleges are finding, in fact, that many people, especially retirees, are interested in learning for learning's sake and not for credit.

This attitude of learning for learning's sake is a valuable asset to students of all ages and is not inconsistent with rigorous academic expectations. People who have a sense that they are learning for their own interest, to broaden their horizons, are usually *engaged* learners. Willingness to experiment, to dabble, to be a beginner, and to explore are all important elements of a healthy recreational approach.

Intercultural Experiences

Despite all the work that has been done to promote integration and awareness, racism and sexism are still deeply entrenched in our culture. Most of the young people the Institute works with come from areas that are still quite segregated and often actively racist and where attitudes toward roles for men and women are often sexist. We believe that to break down race and gender stereotypes, several conditions must be present:

- Young people need to get to know one another in substantive, interactive ways.

- A shared culture must be created, one that respects each member's original culture but at the same time promotes open-mindedness, experimentation, and the possibility of new roles for each participant.

- The barriers to racial mixing and gender mixing must be somehow suspended or broken down.

- Traditional hierarchies must be abandoned and new value systems promoted that value each person's contributions equally.

- Admirable role models who defy stereotypes must be provided: women who use construction tools and enjoy math, men who are emotionally attuned and interested in the arts.

At the Institute, these principles underlie everything that happens; the setting *structurally* mitigates against racist and sexist tendencies by constantly mixing races and genders, by promoting inclusiveness in all parts of the program, by encouraging all participants to experiment with new behaviors, by hiring a multiethnic staff that is multiculturally aware and attentive to these issues, and by removing penalties for failure or mistakes.

As anyone who has tried to create a multicultural setting knows, it takes more than bringing various ethnic or racial groups together to break down segregationist behaviors. In academic settings, it is not unusual to go into the cafeteria, for example, and see tables made up exclusively of African-Americans, or Caucasians, or females, or males. In classrooms with open seating, it is not unusual to see the races and genders segregating themselves as well.

At the Institute, however, a visitor will notice something markedly different: There appears to be no segregation. In leisure times and in programmed activities, groups mixed by race and gender are seen everywhere, focused together on common interests and active pursuits. The environment reinforces and supports this mixing. Not only are students intentionally integrated in room groups, table groups, and evening program groups; they also become randomly—and naturally—integrated as they select activities according to their individual interests. (The sign-up process is designed in such a way that students do not generally know who else is signing up for activities when they make their choices.)

At the Institute, the limits on typical teenage culture set the stage for students to experience something different. They cannot easily fall back on old habits. They are too busy to "hang out" in the groupings they are familiar with; they are openly encouraged to get to know each member of the community in the course of the month;

they have frequent occasions, such as in evening programs and at meal times, to be part of and interact with the whole community; they are challenged to exceed the limits of their previous expectations; and they are away from the influence of media, neighborhood gangs, and others who might pressure them to act "cool" and stay among their "own kind."

As the program swings into gear, a special Institute vocabulary begins to evolve. Terms such as *SST, COD,* and *room group* take on meaning. Shared language is a powerful unifying factor. Added to this is shared humor. Special Institute-wide in-jokes rapidly arise— as counselors or students make amusing comments at just the right time, as group efforts go awry and become amusing anecdotes for the whole community, as room groups or evening program groups share humorous stories.

Also drawing students together are the shared moments of poignancy, awakening, breakthrough, conflict resolution, and insight that give each participant a sense of belonging to the evolving community. As these shared moments are reported, reflected on, and celebrated in conversations and in art, dance, and music presentations, their value is reinforced.

Because of the constant choice and variety of activities available, students have opportunities not only to discover their own interests and passions but also to discover the interests they have in common with others. When Monette (an inner-city African-American student) worked with Mike (a rural white student) to get certified on the lathe, for example, she gained insight into a person she might not have even bothered with back home. Once they had this learning experience in common and had experienced this positive exchange, she discovered he was really quite nice, and he discovered the same about her. As the session progressed, each of them had a new way to interpret and perceive the behaviors and contributions of the other. This small rapprochement is repeated again and again throughout the month-long session as students mix and remix and get to know one another.

The shared activities of the Institute and the schedules that students soon master and use to accomplish their own goals empower the participants. Because everyone shares in this empowerment, individuals have less need for power over others. They have less of a need to put others down to make themselves feel more powerful. They also do not need to defer to others who are humiliating them. This is an exhilarating experience for young people whose home experience is often one of feeling degraded because of their low social status.

Finally, staff members work hard to break down the patterns of conversation and behavior that lead to racism, sexism, and segregation. They encourage young people to see how harmful exclusive conversations can be, how forming couples can exclude or pressure others, how in-jokes that are not shared with others create haves and have-nots. Staff members use the Institute expectations as a basis for helping students to behave more consciously and more considerately toward one another. They model inclusiveness and open-mindedness in all that they do.

Teenagers need to think through issues of sexism and racism for themselves and confront the attitudes they were raised with or have learned in their schools. In such a different environment, where every day they are getting new insights and experiences with one another, they are able to break through some of the social barriers to friendship and racial understanding.

As they try new activities and experience purposeful groupings, they have a unique opportunity to rethink their prejudices and limiting attitudes, becoming more inclusive and socially aware.

6

Lessons Learned: Beyond the High/Scope Institute Model

A successful program like the High/Scope Institute for IDEAS offers several gifts. First, it helps individual young people experience greater self-confidence and success in their lives. Second, it inspires teachers and teachers-in-training to create dynamic learning experiences in whatever environments they work in. And third, it boosts sponsoring school systems by providing enrichment opportunities for their students. Most important, it stands as a model, offering insights to teachers, youth program directors, school administrators, funders, and policymakers who seek to create supportive and effective learning communities for teenagers.

As early as 1974, the High/Scope program served as a model for other residential programs. At that time, educators at the Kamehameha schools in Hawaii, impressed with the positive transformations in students they sent to the High/Scope program, established a similar program of their own. To provide a summer enrichment experience to supplement their school-year offerings, the Kamehameha school system worked closely with High/Scope to create a Hawaiian version of the Institute. They sent staff to the High/Scope facility for training, they hired exchange staff from High/Scope, and they called on students who had attended the Michigan program to take leadership roles in creating the kind of engaged community and active learning environment they had experienced. The Kamehameha replication was the first of many experiments in applying to other settings the lessons learned from the special "laboratory" setting of the Institute in Clinton, Michigan.

The Active Learning Program for Schools

A later significant application of the High/Scope approach to working with teenagers took place at Chadsey High School in Detroit. Funded by The Skillman Foundation, the *Active Learning Program for Schools* was a collaborative effort of the staff of Chadsey High School and High/Scope Foundation to adapt the principles of active learning (as practiced at the Institute) to an inner-city high school program serving gifted and talented adolescents.

Over the course of the 1990 academic year, a High/Scope consulting team conducted for Chadsey teachers a series of six workshops dealing with the principles of active learning, interaction styles in the classroom, and student leadership. Between workshops, teachers could try out new ideas from the workshops in their classrooms. The success of the project was evaluated through questionnaires completed by the teachers and through classroom observations conducted by High/Scope staff (Epstein, 1990).

This experience offered some significant insights into the potential of incorporating High/Scope's approach into the secondary school setting. The results of this project, which was more limited in scope than a full-fledged replication, indicated positive shifts for both teachers and students: Students were clearly more actively involved in the classroom, taking greater responsibility for their own learning and acting as mentors for their peers. Teachers found that by sharing their teaching role with students, they could direct more energy toward appreciating students' talents and meeting individual needs.

Equally important, the series of six workshops initiated a process of discussion and problem solving among Chadsey staff members, who were continually confronted by the limitations and pressures of their school environment. Despite their frustrations, teachers found that the active, cooperative learning concepts introduced through the workshops could be successfully adapted to the traditional academic setting and could make a difference with students. The team problem-solving approach taken in the workshops helped support individual teachers in overcoming any obstacles or fears that stood in the way of innovation.

In the final evaluation of the project, changes on several fronts were reported. Students were found to be more involved in their own learning, and their task-related interactions increased. They also grew more comfortable with cooperative learning and more often worked together to solve problems. Students were also reported to be more animated during class, speaking up more and addressing comments both to their peers and to their teachers. Students took more responsibility for their own learning and displayed more pride in their accomplishments.

Other changes involved the teacher's role. Teachers used cooperative learning strategies more flexibly and offered students more real choices. They became clearer about their expectations for students and were more accepting of students' ideas. Teachers also used more divergent questions to encourage thinking skills and made activities more relevant to student interests. Both students and teachers were reported to derive greater enjoyment from school.

Offered as an inservice training program combined with hands on application, the Active Learning Program for Schools demonstrated that aspects of the High/Scope approach can be adapted to other settings, in this case a public high school.

A Model for Replication

While the Kamehameha schools and the Active Learning Program for Schools both represent important extensions of the High/Scope approach beyond the Institute for IDEAS setting, it was not until 1991 that actual replication of the entire Institute program became a priority and was undertaken as a goal of the Adolescent Division at the High/Scope Foundation. An important catalyst for this replication project was the release of the findings from a longitudinal study conducted with participants from the 1982 and 1983 Institute sessions five years after their programs ended. The findings, reported in *Challenging the Potential: Programs for Talented Disadvantaged Youth* (Oden, Kelly, Ma, & Weikart, 1992), demonstrated the long-term positive impacts the experience had on teenagers. The five-year follow-up of Institute participants assessed their experiences and achievement in education and work; their sources of economic support; their attitudes toward self, work, and education; their perceived sources of influence; and their future goals and plans.

The major finding of the longitudinal study was that compared with a group of economically disadvantaged students who did not attend the Institute, Institute participants reached higher levels of education. After high school, 73 percent of all the High/Scope Institute participants, versus 55 percent of the comparison group, went on to postsecondary education. The most dramatic results, however, were found among those Institute participants who had experienced no special recognition for achievement in high school; of these so-called "nonrecognized achievers," 65 percent went on to postsecondary education. This compared with only 29 percent of their counterparts in the comparison group.

These impressive results led to the establishment of the High/Scope Institute as a national model for replication. In 1991 the DeWitt Wallace–Reader's Digest Fund supported High/Scope's work with adolescents with a development grant for expansion and replication of the High/Scope Institute for IDEAS.

The purpose of the replication grant was to bring High/Scope's residential intervention program to a wide variety of communities, to reach an increased number of teenagers as well as adults who work with teens. In some cases, the High/Scope training and program structure is being used to enhance a currently existing residential program; at other replication sites, teams comprising local officials, schools, students, parents, and youth-serving organizations have formed and are working together to create what will be entirely new programs. "West Virginia—Camp Horseshoe" illustrates one type of replication model.

Beyond Replication: Implications for the Field

The High/Scope longitudinal research study illustrates the potential impact of high-quality intervention programs on the achievement of disadvantaged teenagers. High/Scope's Adolescent Division provides technical assistance and training to a variety of youth-serving

WEST VIRGINIA—CAMP HORSESHOE

Camp Horseshoe, located on 42 acres of the Monongahela National Forest in the small town of St. George, West Virginia, is the site of the nation's first statewide replication of the High/Scope Institute for IDEAS.

The Ohio–West Virginia YMCA, which owns and operates Camp Horseshoe, has been serving West Virginia's youth since 1909 through a variety of successful leadership and youth service programs. Since taking on sponsorship of the Institute replication project, the YMCA has built a network that includes each school district in the state, the Governor's office, the State Department of Education, and local Job Training Partnership Act (JTPA) officials.

What this network is engaged in is much more than replicating a camp program; their efforts thus far constitute a statewide education reform effort that uses the High/Scope Institute for IDEAS as a vehicle for addressing critical issues for the West Virginia schools, including how to deal with at-risk behaviors as well as adolescent development and achievement in general.

The West Virginia program is a sound educational implementation of the Institute. Students are released from school throughout the spring and fall to attend Camp Horseshoe's month-long Institutes. This is possible because the program has been recognized by the local board of education as an Exemption A School (alternative school), indicating its educational value for the population it serves. The program targets low-income ninth- and tenth-graders whose achievement, according to school personnel, does not match their potential. While at the program, students are involved in active, cooperative learning experiences that promote personal growth and problem solving in the arts and in academics. These are very similar to the experiences offered at High/Scope's model program in Clinton, Michigan.

The daily routine implemented at the West Virginia site is similar to that of High/Scope's model. After staff from West Virginia participated in High/Scope training and visited the model program in Clinton, a staff training week parallel to that of the High/Scope model was developed and implemented at Camp Horseshoe.

Student response to West Virginia's replication of the High/Scope Institute has been positive. These are some quotes from students who reflected on the experience during a follow-up retreat:

I love this place. Everyone is so nice. We all work together and care about each other. I found out who I am, that I have good ideas, and that I can be whatever I want. I would live here forever. I just want the rest of my world to

Continued on next page

WEST VIRGINIA—CAMP HORSESHOE continued

be like this place. If we could all care about each other, help each other be our best, and work together, just think how great our schools would be. I'm trying harder in school. I want to succeed. (Lorrie)

• • •

My grades were D's when I came to the Institute. I went home wanting to do better. Now I'm getting B's. I also didn't get along too well with my stepmother. One of my goals was to get along better with her. I made the effort and she responded. Things are really better at my home now. I also feel good about myself. . . . No longer do I do what I think others want me to do. I can be myself and feel good about it. (Stormie)

Outreach to students *following* the Institute is an important part of the replication effort in West Virginia. Students are invited to continue their involvement through participation in other programs offered by the local YMCA, including leadership development and volunteer community service. Students are also followed up through discussions and activities with the Institute's outreach director. Also, the YMCA offers assistance to parents in helping their teens continue the progress made at the Institute and assistance to students in seeking postsecondary educational opportunities as well as financial aid. As has occurred at times in High/Scope's model program, area teachers have opportunities to become involved in the Institute and to work with their students in this unique setting.

organizations interested in applying High/Scope's approach to working with adolescents within their own programs and settings. Officials at prisons and youth detention centers have inquired about ways to adapt some of the living and learning principles to their settings. In Michigan and Texas, workers at residential housing projects have requested and received training in High/Scope's active learning approach to working with adolescents. Teachers from various school systems have requested training in implementing active learning and cooperative learning.

It is especially interesting to see how diverse organizations that work with adolescents can benefit from specific aspects of the High/Scope model. Some are particularly interested in learning how to increase the benefits of teenagers' nonformal interaction times, for example. Others want to know how they might rethink and restructure formal instructional settings for greater student initiative, collaboration, and active learning.

In an effort to make High/Scope experiences and practices accessible to a diverse group of program providers, the High/Scope Foundation has developed consulting processes and training materials that can enhance the work of a range of youth professionals. We believe that the Institute's approach to working with teenagers has applications for the following: staff in other residential settings, school administrators and teachers, adults overseeing school extracurricular activities, parents and families, youth service organizations, job-training programs, and the juvenile justice system.

Staff in other residential settings can use the information about room groups and nonformal times and about group dynamics to help them build community. The information on adult-student interactions and dealing with disruptive behaviors can be helpful in situations where maintaining discipline seems to take up more staff energy than programming does.

School administrators can benefit from ideas on how to create a system that includes more autonomy and initiative on the part of students. The information on community building, on fostering leadership, and on making learning more active and cooperative can help schools make better use of both students' and teachers' talents.

Individual classroom teachers can implement principles of active learning, cooperative learning, and student mentoring, even within an otherwise traditional school structure.

Adults overseeing school extracurricular activities, such as sports, choirs, and drama clubs, can be strengthened with insights about inspiring cooperation, supporting exploration of concepts and ideas, helping students mentor and encourage one another, and structuring activities so individuals can participate on their own terms and discover their own particular strengths.

Parents and families can draw from the strategies for supporting their teenager's positive development through improved communication and conflict resolution. They can also learn how to work in their families or community groups to strengthen their teenager's experience of positive group living and to promote active and constructive recreation.

Youth service organizations can implement aspects of the educational approach, in particular the plan-do-review process, to strengthen the activities they offer. They can also draw on the strategies for fostering cooperative learning while ensuring each individual's engaged participation.

Job-training programs can integrate the Institute's approaches to building community, promoting personal responsibility, providing purposeful work, setting career goals, integrating work with learning, and building self-confidence through programming that allows participants to experience regular, meaningful success.

The juvenile justice system can benefit from the Institute's success with helping young people define and pursue meaningful activities, build self-confidence through positive actions, and develop an understanding of how their behaviors affect others. The practices implemented at the Institute create an environment of caring and involvement; individuals who have been difficult to reach at school and in other settings can discover new aspects to their character and new strengths.

Implications for Youth Policy

Promoting the higher education of disadvantaged students is a key step in increasing the leadership of the future. Oden and others (1992) in *Challenging the Potential* emphasized the importance of taking this step:

> The potential of our nation's talented disadvantaged and minority youth too often goes unrealized. The United States, though enriched by the diversity in religion, race, national origin, and cultural background among its people, has always faced a challenge in providing each citizen with adequate opportunity in education and employment. Today the challenge presented by diversity remains undiminished. And today, because of the vast changes that have occurred in the American workplace and family over the past 20 years, we face a new kind of challenge. Perhaps more than ever before, it is imperative

nteresting impli-
other groups
eral education
ing funds draw
pe's experiences
ore effective
or young people?
3 the U.S.
of Labor and
artment of
iblished *The
Basic Skills in the*
his document set
ies regarding
training pro-
esting that they
nly foster higher
nic skills, prob-
and decision
ilso include prob-
situations and
t require using
nportant in the
Although typical
," (programs
develop job
ng people) often
fferent from the
he Institute for
i/Scope's longitu-
h has shown
d goals of high-
aining can be
gaged commu-

igitudinal study
impact after

rage and
ng people

iin, the empirical
ata on the Institute's
n programs to fur-
rticularly in terms of
emic performance
he benefit of strong
motivated to go on
ion by such students
act. Among the
ir expected income
nents for their fami-
condary education
358). And, when
n their greater pro-

vide range of goals
citizens, including
nply seeking to
viors, society should
opment of youth.
oblem behaviors
ise or teenage preg-
ild be focused on
ople from a positive,
ocate adequate
outh—we must
orograms are effec-
or preventing
ng level must take
anded to include

IDEAS have been
ining Partnership
ual use of these

Students' relationships to peers and community are strengthened through positive, collaborative work experiences that require individual and collective responsibility and problem solving.

funds with
cations. Ca
receiving fe
and job-trai
on High/Sc
to provide
enrichment

In 19
Departmen
the U.S. De
Education
Bottom Line
Workplace.
general pol
high-quality
grams, sugg
should not
order acade
lem solving
making but
lem-solving
activities th
basic skills
workplace.
"job trainin
designed to
skills in you
look very d
program at
IDEAS, Hig
dinal resea
that the bro
quality job

achieved through cooperative active learning and e
nity, as practiced at the High/Scope Institute.

Through several path analyses done on the l
data to determine the factors that created long-term

such a short-term intervention, several key processes that students went through at the Institute were clearly highlighted:

- Role model influences at the Institute positively affected students' expectations and motivation for achievement, as well as their relationship with authority figures.

- Students' active academic experience was strengthened at the Institute as they tried various problem-solving strategies, identified obstacles, experimented with solutions, planned tasks, and reviewed the outcomes.

- Students' relationships to peers and community (important in most work situations) were strengthened through their experiences with collaborative work, their contact with cultural diversity, and their concrete experience of taking individual responsibility within the community context.

Interestingly, both JTPA and Chapter One evaluations have coincided in determining that many of their current programs for youth fail to provide exposure to these processes. Although programs that teach adolescents specific job-related skills are extremely important, being able to type is of little consequence to an individual who does not take responsibility for personal behavior, who does not feel much self-worth, or who has few interpersonal skills.

Programs that are effective are those that reach beyond developing narrow skills and treating or preventing destructive behaviors. Effective programs—like the Institute for IDEAS—treat young people as whole individuals, helping them to build skills and to set goals. They provide teenagers with opportunities to develop their potential and become contributing members of their communities.

References

Bronfenbrenner, U. (1979). *The ecology of human development: Experiments by nature and design.* Cambridge, MA: Harvard University Press.

Case, R. (1985). *Intellectual development: Birth to adulthood.* New York: Academic Press.

Dorman, G. (1981). *Middle Grades Assessment Program: User's manual.* Carrboro, NC: Center for Early Adolescence, University of North Carolina at Chapel Hill.

Dorman, G., & Lipsitz, J. (1984). Early adolescent development. In G. Dorman (Ed.), *Middle Grades Assessment Program: User's manual* (Chapter 2). Carrboro, NC: Center for Early Adolescence, University of North Carolina at Chapel Hill.

Elliot, G. R., & Feldman, S. S. (1990). Capturing the adolescent experience. In S. S. Feldman & G. R. Elliot (Eds.), *At the threshold: The developing adolescent* (pp. 1–13). Cambridge, MA: Harvard University Press.

Epstein, A. (1990, Spring/Summer). Applying strategies from High/Scope camp to an inner-city gifted and talented high school program. *High/Scope ReSource,* p. 1.

Erikson, E. H. (1963). *Childhood and society* (2nd ed.). New York: Norton.

Erikson, E. H. (1968). *Identity, youth, and crisis.* New York: Norton.

Keating, D. P. (1990). Adolescent thinking. In S. S. Feldman & G R. Elliot (Eds.), *At the threshold: The developing adolescent* (pp. 54–89). Cambridge, MA: Harvard University Press.

Lefstein, L. M., & Lipsitz, J. (1986). *3:00 to 6:00 PM: Programs for young adolescents.* Carrboro, NC: Center for Early Adolescence, University of North Carolina at Chapel Hill.

Lewis, A., & Smith, D. (1993, Summer). Defining higher order thinking. *Theory into Practice, 32* (3), 131–137.

Oden, S., Kelly, M. A., Ma, Z., & Weikart, D. P. (1992). *Challenging the potential: Programs for talented disadvantaged youth.* Ypsilanti, MI: High/Scope Press.

Piaget, J. (1972). Intellectual evaluation from adolescence to adulthood. *Human Development, 15,* 1–2.

Pittman, K. J., & Wright, M. (1991). *A rationale for enhancing the role of the non-school voluntary sector in youth development* (Research Paper No. 1). Washington, DC: Center for Youth Development and Policy Research, Academy for Educational Development.

Schine, J. (1990, Spring). A rationale for youth community service. *Social Policy, 20* (4), 5–12.

Schweinhart, L. J., Barnes, H. V., & Weikart, D. P. (1993). *The High/Scope Perry Preschool study through age 27* (Monographs of the High/Scope Educational Research Foundation, 10). Ypsilanti, MI: High/Scope Press.

Sullivan, J. S. (1953). *The interpersonal theory of psychiatry.* New York: Norton.

Tishman, S., Jay, E., & Perkins, D. N. (1993, Summer). Teaching thinking dispositions: From transmission to enculturation. *Theory into Practice, 32*(3), 147–153.

Underbakke, M., Borg, J. M., & Peterson, D. (1993, Summer). Researching and developing the knowledge base for teaching higher order thinking. *Theory into Practice, 32*(3), 138–146.

U.S. Department of Labor & U.S. Department of Education. (1988). *The bottom line: Basic skills in the workplace.* Washington, DC: Author.

Zeldin, S. (1993, September). *Professional development of youth workers: What is best practice?* (First Year Report: "Professional Development of Youth Workers"). Washington, DC: Center for Youth Development and Policy Research, Academy for Educational Development.

Index

Ohio-West Virginia YMCA, 205
Open-ended questioning. *See* Divergent questioning
Open framework, 6, 46, 74, 118–19, 121
Opening activity, 110, 122–23, 135–36, 142

P

Participation, 100
Peer teaching, 141, 149
Perkins, D. N., 177, 178
Peterson, D., 173, 177
Piaget, Jean, 30, 33
Pittman, Karen J., xi–xv, 40, 42, 44, 45, 186, 192, 196
Plan-do-review, 15, 110, 115, 120, 122, 128–30, 136–37, 172, 177
Presentations, 60–61
Problem-solving skills, 150–51, 190–91
Program schedule, 46–47
Psychotherapy, 96

R

"A Rationale for Youth Community Service," (Schine), 166
"Researching and Developing the Knowledge Base for Teaching
        Higher Order Thinking," (Underbakke, Borg, & Peterson), 173
Role models, 22, 184, 195, 211
Room groups, 55–56, 69, 190, 199
Room time, 55, 56–57
Rules and policies, 97–99

S

Safe environment, 21, 93, 95–97
    and program, 95–96
Salcau, Jane, xx
Salcau, John, xx
Schine, Joan, 166
School, as a cultural vacuum, 38
Self-scheduled time, 17, 67, 143, 193, 199
Service-learning, 166, 169, 170, 172
    projects, 174–75

About the Author

Ellen Meredith Ilfeld is an alumna of High/Scope s summer program for teenagers. As a former camper, counselor, and Foundation staff member, she has tried to convey here the experience and feel of the High/Scope Institute for IDEAS, as well as its curriculum. Ellen has a Doctor of Arts degree in Writing from the University of Michigan. She has taught writing at several universities and at present owns a small publishing company and edits an international journal on early childhood care and development. She is coauthor, with Judith Evans, of *Good Beginnings: Parenting in the Early Years* (High/Scope Press). Using the pen name Ellen Meredith, she is author of *Listening In: Dialogues with the Wiser Self* (Horse Mountain Press).